Fundamental Princi_

Of The

Metaphysic Of Morals

&

The

Metaphysical Elements

Of

Ethics

by

Immanuel Kant

translated by
Thomas Kingsmill Abbott

Table of Contents

Fundamental Principles

Of The

Metaphysic Of Morals

by

Immanuel Kant

translated by
Thomas Kingsmill Abbott

PREFACE

Ancient Greek philosophy was divided into three sciences: physics, ethics, and logic. This division is perfectly suitable to the nature of the thing; and the only improvement that can be made in it is to add the principle on which it is based, so that we may both satisfy ourselves of its completeness, and also be able to determine correctly the necessary subdivisions.

All rational knowledge is either material or formal: the former considers some object, the latter is concerned only with the form of the understanding and of the reason itself, and with the universal laws of thought in general without distinction of its objects. Formal philosophy is called logic. Material philosophy, however, has to do with determinate objects and the laws to which they are subject, is again twofold; for these laws are either laws of nature or of freedom. The science of the former is physics, that of the latter, ethics; they are also called natural philosophy and moral philosophy respectively.

Logic cannot have any empirical part; that is, a part in which the universal and necessary laws of thought should rest on grounds taken from experience; otherwise it would not be logic, *i.e.*, a canon for the understanding or the reason, valid for all thought, and capable of demonstration. Natural and moral philosophy, on the contrary, can each have their empirical part, since the former has to determine the laws of nature as an object of experience; the latter the laws of the human will, so far as it is affected by nature: the former, however, being laws according to which everything does happen; the latter, laws according to which everything ought to happen. Ethics, however, must also consider the conditions under which what ought to happen frequently does not.

We may call all philosophy empirical, so far as it is based on grounds of experience: on the other band, that which delivers its doctrines from a priori principles alone we may call pure philosophy. When the latter is merely formal it is logic; if it is restricted to definite objects of the understanding it is metaphysic.

In this way there arises the idea of a twofold metaphysic- a metaphysic of nature and a metaphysic of morals. Physics will thus have an empirical and also a rational part. It is the same with Ethics; but here the empirical part might have the special name of practical anthropology, the name morality being appropriated to the rational part.

All trades, arts, and handiworks have gained by division of labour, namely, when, instead of one man doing everything, each confines himself to a certain kind of work distinct from others in the treatment it requires, so as to be able to perform it with greater facility and in the greatest perfection. Where the different kinds of work are not distinguished and divided, where everyone is a jack-of-all-trades, there manufactures remain still in the greatest barbarism. It might deserve to be considered whether pure philosophy in all its parts does not require a man specially devoted to it, and whether it would not be better for the whole business of science if those who, to please the tastes of the public, are wont to blend the rational and empirical elements together, mixed in all sorts of proportions unknown to themselves, and who call themselves independent thinkers, giving the name of minute philosophers to those who apply themselves to the rational part only- if these, I say, were warned not to carry on two employments together which differ widely in the treatment they demand, for each of which perhaps a special talent is required, and the combination of which in one person only produces bunglers. But I only ask here whether the nature of science does not require that we should always carefully separate the empirical from the rational part, and prefix to Physics proper (or empirical physics) a metaphysic of nature, and to practical anthropology a metaphysic of morals, which must be carefully cleared of everything empirical, so that we may know how much can be accomplished by pure reason in both cases, and from what sources it draws this its a priori teaching, and that whether the latter inquiry is conducted by all moralists (whose name is legion), or only by some who feel a calling thereto.

As my concern here is with moral philosophy, I limit the question suggested to this: Whether it is not of the utmost necessity to construct a pure thing which is only empirical and which belongs to anthropology? for that such a philosophy must be possible is evident from the common idea of duty and of the moral laws. Everyone must admit that if a law is to have moral force, *i.e.*, to be the basis of an obligation, it must carry with it absolute necessity; that, for example, the precept, "Thou shalt not lie," is not valid for men alone, as if other rational beings had no need to observe it; and so with all the other moral laws properly so called; that, therefore, the basis of obligation must not be sought in the nature of man, or in the circumstances in the world in which he is placed, but a priori simply in the conception of pure reason; and although any other precept which is founded on principles of mere experience may be in certain respects universal, yet in as far as it rests even in the least degree on an empirical basis, perhaps only as to a motive, such a precept, while it may be a practical rule, can never be called a moral law.

Thus not only are moral laws with their principles essentially distinguished from every other kind of practical knowledge in which there is anything empirical, but all moral philosophy rests wholly on its pure part. When applied to man, it does not borrow the least thing from the knowledge of man himself (anthropology), but gives laws a priori to him as a rational being. No doubt these laws require a judgement sharpened by experience, in order on the one hand to distinguish in what cases they are applicable, and on the other to procure for them access to the will of the man and effectual influence on conduct; since man is acted on by so many inclinations that, though capable of the idea of a practical pure reason, he is not so easily able to make it effective in *concreto* in his life.

A metaphysic of morals is therefore indispensably necessary, not merely for speculative reasons, in order to investigate the sources of the practical principles which are to be found a priori in our reason, but also because morals themselves are liable to all sorts of corruption, as long as we are without that clue and supreme canon by which to estimate them correctly. For in order that an action should be morally good, it is not enough that it conform to the moral law, but it must also be done for the sake of the law, otherwise that conformity is only very contingent and uncertain; since a principle which is not moral, although it may now and then produce actions conformable to the law, will also often produce actions which contradict it. Now it is only a pure philosophy that we can look for the moral law in its purity and genuineness (and, in a practical matter, this is of the utmost consequence): we must, therefore, begin with pure philosophy (metaphysic), and without it there cannot be any moral philosophy at all. That which mingles these pure principles with the empirical does not deserve the name of philosophy (for what distinguishes philosophy from common rational knowledge is that it treats in separate sciences what the latter only comprehends confusedly); much less does it deserve that of moral philosophy, since by this confusion it even spoils the purity of morals themselves, and counteracts its own end.

Let it not be thought, however, that what is here demanded is already extant in the propaedeutic prefixed by the celebrated Wolf to his moral philosophy, namely, his so-called general practical philosophy, and that, therefore, we have not to strike into an entirely new field. Just because it was to be a general practical philosophy, it has not taken into consideration a will of any particular kind- say one which should be determined solely from a priori principles without any empirical motives, and which we might call a pure will, but volition in general, with all the actions and conditions which belong to it in this general signification. By this it is distinguished from a metaphysic of morals, just as general logic, which treats of the acts and canons of thought in general, is distinguished from transcendental philosophy, which treats of the particular acts and canons of pure thought, i.e., that whose cognitions are altogether a priori. For the metaphysic of morals has to examine the idea and the principles of a possible pure will, and not the acts and conditions of human volition generally, which for the most part are drawn from psychology. It is true that moral laws and duty are spoken of in the general moral philosophy (contrary indeed to all fitness). But this is no objection, for in this respect also the authors of that science remain true to their idea of it; they do not distinguish the motives which are prescribed as such by reason alone altogether a priori, and which are properly moral, from the empirical motives which the understanding raises to general conceptions merely by comparison of experiences; but, without noticing the difference of their sources, and looking on them all as homogeneous, they consider only their greater or less amount. It is in this way they frame their notion of obligation, which, though anything but moral, is all that can be attained in a philosophy which passes no judgement at all on the origin of all possible practical concepts, whether they are a priori, or only a posteriori.

Intending to publish hereafter a metaphysic of morals, I issue in the first instance these fundamental principles. Indeed there is properly no other foundation for it than the critical examination of a pure practical Reason; just as that of metaphysics is the critical examination of the pure speculative reason, already published. But in the first place the former is not so absolutely necessary as the latter, because in moral concerns human reason can easily be brought to a high degree of correctness and completeness, even in the commonest understanding, while on the contrary in its theoretic but pure use it is wholly dialectical; and in the second place if the critique of a pure practical reason is to be complete, it must be possible at the same time to show its identity with the speculative reason in a common principle, for it can ultimately be only one and the same reason which has to be distinguished merely in its application. I could not, however, bring it to such completeness here, without introducing considerations of a wholly different kind, which would be perplexing to the reader. On this account I have adopted the title of Fundamental Principles of the Metaphysic of Morals instead of that of a Critical Examination of the pure practical reason.

But in the third place, since a metaphysic of morals, in spite of the discouraging title, is yet capable of being presented in popular form, and one adapted to the common understanding, I find it useful to separate from it this preliminary treatise on its fundamental principles, in order that I may not hereafter have need to introduce these necessarily subtle discussions into a book of a more simple character.

The present treatise is, however, nothing more than the investigation and establishment of the supreme principle of morality, and this alone constitutes a study complete in itself and one which ought to be kept apart from every other moral investigation. No doubt my conclusions on this weighty question, which has hitherto been very unsatisfactorily examined, would receive much light from the application of the same principle to the whole system, and would be greatly confirmed by the adequacy which it exhibits throughout; but I must forego this advantage, which indeed would be after all more gratifying than useful, since the easy applicability of a principle and its apparent adequacy give no very certain proof of its soundness, but rather inspire a certain partiality, which prevents us from examining and estimating it strictly in itself and without regard to consequences.

I have adopted in this work the method which I think most suitable, proceeding analytically from common knowledge to the determination of its ultimate principle, and again descending synthetically from the examination of this principle and its sources to the common knowledge in which we find it employed. The division will, therefore, be as follows:

1 FIRST SECTION. Transition from the common rational knowledge of morality to the philosophical.

2 SECOND SECTION. Transition from popular moral philosophy to the metaphysic of morals.

3 THIRD SECTION. Final step from the metaphysic of morals to the critique of the pure practical reason.

First Section

Transition From The Common Rational Knowledge
Of Morality To The Philosophical

Nothing can possibly be conceived in the world, or even out of it, which can be called good, without qualification, except a good will. Intelligence, wit, judgement, and the other talents of the mind, however they may be named, or courage, resolution, perseverance, as qualities of temperament, are undoubtedly good and desirable in many respects; but these gifts of nature may also become extremely bad and mischievous if the will which is to make use of them, and which, therefore, constitutes what is called character, is not good. It is the same with the gifts of fortune. Power, riches, honour, even health, and the general well-being and contentment with one's condition which is called happiness, inspire pride, and often presumption, if there is not a good will to correct the influence of these on the mind, and with this also to rectify the whole principle of acting and adapt it to its end. The sight of a being who is not adorned with a single feature of a pure and good will, enjoying unbroken prosperity, can never give pleasure to an impartial rational spectator. Thus a good will appears to constitute the indispensable condition even of being worthy of happiness.

There are even some qualities which are of service to this good will itself and may facilitate its action, yet which have no intrinsic unconditional value, but always presuppose a good will, and this qualifies the esteem that we justly have for them and does not permit us to regard them as absolutely good. Moderation in the affections and passions, self-control, and calm deliberation are not only good in many respects, but even seem to constitute part of the intrinsic worth of the person; but they are far from deserving to be called good without qualification, although they have been so unconditionally praised by the ancients. For without the principles of a good will, they may become extremely bad, and the coolness of a villain not only makes him far more dangerous, but also directly makes him more abominable in our eyes than he would have been without it.

A good will is good not because of what it performs or effects, not by its aptness for the attainment of some proposed end, but simply by virtue of the volition; that is, it is good in itself, and considered by itself is to be esteemed much higher than all that can be brought about by it in favour of any inclination, nay even of the sum total of all inclinations. Even if it should happen that, owing to special disfavour of fortune, or the niggardly provision of a step-motherly nature, this will should wholly lack power to accomplish its purpose, if with its greatest efforts it should yet achieve nothing, and there should remain only the good will (not, to be sure, a mere wish, but the summoning of all means in our power), then, like a jewel, it would still shine by its own light, as a thing which has its whole value in itself. Its usefulness or fruitlessness can neither add nor take away anything from this value. It would be, as it were, only the setting to enable us to handle it the more conveniently in common commerce, or to attract to it the attention of those who are not yet connoisseurs, but not to recommend it to true connoisseurs, or to determine its value.

There is, however, something so strange in this idea of the absolute value of the mere will, in which no account is taken of its utility, that notwithstanding the thorough assent of even common reason to the idea, yet a suspicion must arise that it may perhaps really be the product of mere high-flown fancy, and that we may have misunderstood the purpose of nature in assigning reason as the governor of our will. Therefore we will examine this idea from this point of view.

In the physical constitution of an organized being, that is, a being adapted suitably to the purposes of life, we assume it as a fundamental principle that no organ for any purpose will be found but what is also the fittest and best adapted for that purpose. Now in a being which has reason and a will, if the proper object of nature were its conservation, its welfare, in a word, its happiness, then nature would have hit upon a very bad arrangement in selecting the reason of the creature to carry out this purpose. For all the actions which the creature has to perform with a view to this purpose, and the whole rule of its conduct, would be far more surely prescribed to it by instinct, and that end would have been attained thereby much more certainly than it ever can be by reason. Should reason have been communicated to this favored creature over and above, it must only have served it to contemplate the happy constitution of its nature, to admire it, to congratulate itself thereon, and to feel thankful for it to the beneficent cause, but not that it should subject its desires to that weak and delusive guidance and meddle bunglingly with the purpose of nature. In a word, nature would have taken care that reason should not break forth into practical exercise, nor have the presumption, with its weak insight, to think out for itself the plan of happiness, and of the means of attaining it. Nature would not only have taken on herself the choice of the ends, but also of the means, and with wise foresight would have entrusted both to instinct.

And, in fact, we find that the more a cultivated reason applies itself with deliberate purpose to the enjoyment of life and happiness, so much the more does the man fail of true satisfaction. And from this circumstance there arises in many, if they are candid enough to confess it, a certain degree of misology, that is, hatred of reason, especially in the case of those who are most experienced in the use of it, because after calculating all the advantages they derive, I do not say from the invention of all the arts of common luxury, but even from the sciences (which seem to them to be after all only a luxury of the understanding), they find that they have, in fact, only brought more trouble on their shoulders, rather than gained in happiness; and they end by envying, rather than despising, the more common stamp of men who keep closer to the guidance of mere instinct and do not allow their reason much influence on their conduct. And this we must admit, that the judgement of those who would very much lower the lofty eulogies of the advantages which reason gives us in regard to the happiness and satisfaction of life, or who would even reduce them below zero, is by no means morose or ungrateful to the goodness with which the world is governed, but that there lies at the root of these judgements the idea that our existence has a different and far nobler end, for which, and not for happiness, reason is properly intended, and which must, therefore, be regarded as the supreme condition to which the private ends of man must, for the most part, be postponed.

For as reason is not competent to guide the will with certainty in regard to its objects and the satisfaction of all our wants (which it to some extent even multiplies), this being an end to which an implanted instinct would have led with much greater certainty; and since, nevertheless, reason is imparted to us as a practical faculty, *i.e.*, as one which is to have influence on the will, therefore, admitting that nature generally in the distribution of her capacities has adapted the means to the end, its true destination must be to produce a will, not merely good as a means to something else, but good in itself, for which reason was absolutely necessary. This will then, though not indeed the sole and complete good, must be the supreme good and the condition of every other, even of the desire of happiness. Under these circumstances, there is nothing inconsistent with the wisdom of nature in the fact that the cultivation of the reason, which is requisite for the first and unconditional purpose, does in many ways interfere, at least in this life, with the attainment of the second, which is always conditional, namely, happiness. Nay, it may even reduce it to nothing, without nature thereby failing of her purpose. For reason recognizes the establishment of a good will as its highest practical destination, and in attaining this purpose is capable only of a satisfaction of its own proper kind, namely that from the attainment of an end, which end again is determined by reason only, notwithstanding that this may involve many a disappointment to the ends of inclination.

We have then to develop the notion of a will which deserves to be highly esteemed for itself and is good without a view to anything further, a notion which exists already in the sound natural understanding, requiring rather to be cleared up than to be taught, and which in estimating the value of our actions always takes the first place and constitutes the condition of all the rest. In order to do this, we will take the notion of duty, which includes that of a good will, although implying certain subjective restrictions and hindrances. These, however, far from concealing it, or rendering it unrecognizable, rather bring it out by contrast and make it shine forth so much the brighter.

I omit here all actions which are already recognized as inconsistent with duty, although they may be useful for this or that purpose, for with these the question whether they are done from duty cannot arise at all, since they even conflict with it. I also set aside those actions which really conform to duty, but to which men have no direct inclination, performing them because they are impelled thereto by some other inclination. For in this case we can readily distinguish whether the action which agrees with duty is done from duty, or from a selfish view. It is much harder to make this distinction when the action accords with duty and the subject has besides a direct inclination to it. For example, it is always a matter of duty that a dealer should not over charge an inexperienced purchaser; and wherever there is much commerce the prudent tradesman does not overcharge, but keeps a fixed price for everyone, so that a child buys of him as well as any other. Men are thus honestly served; but this is not enough to make us believe that the tradesman has so acted from duty and from principles of honesty: his own advantage required it; it is out of the question in this case to suppose that he might besides have a direct inclination in favour of the buyers, so that, as it were, from love he should give no advantage to one over another. Accordingly the action was done neither from duty nor from direct inclination, but merely with a selfish view.

On the other hand, it is a duty to maintain one's life; and, in addition, everyone has also a direct inclination to do so. But on this account of anxious care, which most men take for it, has no intrinsic worth, and their maxim has no moral import. They preserve their life as duty requires, no doubt, but not because duty requires. On the other band, if adversity and hopeless sorrow have completely taken away the relish for life; if the unfortunate one, strong in mind, indignant at his fate rather than desponding or dejected, wishes for death, and yet preserves his life without loving it- not from inclination or fear, but from duty- then his maxim has a moral worth.

To be beneficent when we can is a duty; and besides this, there are many minds so sympathetically constituted that, without any other motive of vanity or self-interest, they find a pleasure in spreading joy around them and can take delight in the satisfaction of others so far as it is their own work. But I maintain that in such a case an action of this kind, however proper, however amiable it may be, has nevertheless no true moral worth, but is on a level with other inclinations, e.g., the inclination to honour, which, if it is happily directed to that which is in fact of public utility and accordant with duty and consequently honourable, deserves praise and encouragement, but not esteem. For the maxim lacks the moral import, namely, that such actions be done from duty, not from inclination. Put the case that the mind of that philanthropist were clouded by sorrow of his own, extinguishing all sympathy with the lot of others, and that, while he still has the power to benefit others in distress, he is not touched by their trouble because he is absorbed with his own; and now suppose that he tears himself out of this dead insensibility, and performs the action without any inclination to it, but simply from duty, then first has his action its genuine moral worth. Further still; if nature has put little sympathy in the heart of this or that man; if he, supposed to be an upright man, is by temperament cold and indifferent to the sufferings of others, perhaps because in respect of his own he is provided with the special gift of patience and fortitude and supposes, or even requires, that others should have the same- and such a man would certainly not be the meanest product of nature- but if nature had not specially framed him for a philanthropist, would he not still find in himself a source from whence to give himself a far higher worth than that of a good-natured temperament could be? Unquestionably. It is just in this that the moral worth of the character is brought out which is incomparably the highest of all, namely, that he is beneficent, not from inclination, but from duty.

To secure one's own happiness is a duty, at least indirectly; for discontent with one's condition, under a pressure of many anxieties and amidst unsatisfied wants, might easily become a great temptation to transgression of duty. But here again, without looking to duty, all men have already the strongest and most intimate inclination to happiness, because it is just in this idea that all inclinations are combined in one total. But the precept of happiness is often of such a sort that it greatly interferes with some inclinations, and yet a man cannot form any definite and certain conception of the sum of satisfaction of all of them which is called happiness. It is not then to be wondered at that a single inclination, definite both as to what it promises and as to the time within which it can be gratified, is often able to overcome such a fluctuating idea, and that a gouty patient, for instance, can choose to enjoy what he likes, and to suffer what he may, since, according to his calculation, on this occasion at least, he has not sacrificed the enjoyment of the present moment to a possibly mistaken expectation of a happiness which is supposed to be found in health. But even in this case, if the general desire for happiness did not influence his will, and supposing that in his particular case health was not a necessary element in this calculation, there yet remains in this, as in all other cases, this law, namely, that he should promote his happiness not from inclination but from duty, and by this would his conduct first acquire true moral worth.

It is in this manner, undoubtedly, that we are to understand those passages of Scripture also in which we are commanded to love our neighbour, even our enemy. For love, as an affection, cannot be commanded, but beneficence for duty's sake may; even though we are not impelled to it by any inclination- nay, are even repelled by a natural and unconquerable aversion. This is practical love and not pathological- a love which is seated in the will, and not in the propensions of sense- in principles of action and not of tender sympathy; and it is this love alone which can be commanded.

The second proposition is: That an action done from duty derives its moral worth, not from the purpose which is to be attained by it, but from the maxim by which it is determined, and therefore does not depend on the realization of the object of the action, but merely on the principle of volition by which the action has taken place, without regard to any object of desire. It is clear from what precedes that the purposes which we may have in view in our actions, or their effects regarded as ends and springs of the will, cannot give to actions any unconditional or moral worth. In what, then, can their worth lie, if it is not to consist in the will and in reference to its expected effect? It cannot lie anywhere but in the principle of the will without regard to the ends which can be attained by the action. For the will stands between its a priori principle, which is formal, and its a posteriori spring, which is material, as between two roads, and as it must be determined by something, it that it must be determined by the formal principle of volition when an action is done from duty, in which case every material principle has been withdrawn from it.

The third proposition, which is a consequence of the two preceding, I would express thus Duty is the necessity of acting from respect for the law. I may have inclination for an object as the effect of my proposed action, but I cannot have respect for it, just for this reason, that it is an effect and not an energy of will. Similarly I cannot have respect for inclination, whether my own or another's; I can at most, if my own, approve it; if another's, sometimes even love it; i.e., look on it as favourable to my own interest. It is only what is connected with my will as a principle, by no means as an effect- what does not subserve my inclination, but overpowers it, or at least in case of choice excludes it from its calculation- in other words, simply the law of itself, which can be an object of respect, and hence a command. Now an action done from duty must wholly exclude the influence of inclination and with it every object of the will, so that nothing remains which can determine the will except objectively the law, and subjectively pure respect for this practical law, and consequently the maxim[1] that I should follow this law even to the thwarting of all my inclinations.

Thus the moral worth of an action does not lie in the effect expected from it, nor in any principle of action which requires to borrow its motive from this expected effect. For all these effects- agreeableness of one's condition and even the promotion of the happiness of others- could have been also brought about by other causes, so that for this there would have been no need of the will of a rational being; whereas it is in this alone that the supreme and unconditional good can be found. The pre-eminent good which we call moral can therefore consist in nothing else than the conception of law in itself, which certainly is only possible in a rational being, in so far as this conception, and not the expected effect, determines the will. This is a good which is already present in the person who acts accordingly, and we have not to wait for it to appear first in the result.[2]

---

[1] A maxim is the subjective principle of volition. The objective principle (*i.e.*, that which would also serve subjectively as a practical principle to all rational beings if reason had full power over the faculty of desire) is the practical law.

[2] It might be here objected to me that I take refuge behind the word respect in an obscure feeling, instead of giving a distinct solution of the question by a concept of the reason. But although respect is a feeling, it is not a feeling received through influence, but is self-wrought by a rational concept, and, therefore, is specifically distinct from all feelings of the former kind, which may be referred either to inclination or fear. What I recognise immediately as a law for me, I recognise with respect. This merely signifies the consciousness that my will is subordinate to a law, without the intervention of other influences on my sense. The immediate determination of the will by the law, and the consciousness of this, is called respect, so that this is regarded as an effect of the law on the subject, and not as the cause of it. Respect is properly the conception of a worth which thwarts my self-love. Accordingly it is something which is considered neither as an object of inclination nor of fear, although it has something analogous to both. The object of respect is the law only, and that the law which we impose on ourselves and yet recognise as necessary in itself. As a law, we are subjected too it without consulting self-love; as imposed by us on ourselves, it is a result of our will. In the former aspect it has an analogy to fear, in the latter to inclination. Respect for a person is properly only respect for the law (of honesty, etc.) of which he gives us an example. Since we also look on the improvement of our talents as a duty, we consider that we see in a person of talents, as it were, the example of a law (viz., to become like him in this by exercise), and this constitutes our respect. All so-called moral interest consists simply in respect for the law.

But what sort of law can that be, the conception of which must determine the will, even without paying any regard to the effect expected from it, in order that this will may be called good absolutely and without qualification? As I have deprived the will of every impulse which could arise to it from obedience to any law, there remains nothing but the universal conformity of its actions to law in general, which alone is to serve the will as a principle, *i.e.*, I am never to act otherwise than so that I could also will that my maxim should become a universal law. Here, now, it is the simple conformity to law in general, without assuming any particular law applicable to certain actions, that serves the will as its principle and must so serve it, if duty is not to be a vain delusion and a chimerical notion. The common reason of men in its practical judgements perfectly coincides with this and always has in view the principle here suggested. Let the question be, for example: May I when in distress make a promise with the intention not to keep it? I readily distinguish here between the two significations which the question may have: Whether it is prudent, or whether it is right, to make a false promise? The former may undoubtedly of be the case. I see clearly indeed that it is not enough to extricate myself from a present difficulty by means of this subterfuge, but it must be well considered whether there may not hereafter spring from this lie much greater inconvenience than that from which I now free myself, and as, with all my supposed cunning, the consequences cannot be so easily foreseen but that credit once lost may be much more injurious to me than any mischief which I seek to avoid at present, it should be considered whether it would not be more prudent to act herein according to a universal maxim and to make it a habit to promise nothing except with the intention of keeping it. But it is soon clear to me that such a maxim will still only be based on the fear of consequences. Now it is a wholly different thing to be truthful from duty and to be so from apprehension of injurious consequences. In the first case, the very notion of the action already implies a law for me; in the second case, I must first look about elsewhere to see what results may be combined with it which would affect myself. For to deviate from the principle of duty is beyond all doubt wicked; but to be unfaithful to my maxim of prudence may often be very advantageous to me, although to abide by it is certainly safer. The shortest way, however, and an unerring one, to discover the answer to this question whether a lying promise is consistent with duty, is to ask myself, "Should I be content that my maxim (to extricate myself from difficulty by a false promise) should hold good as a universal law, for myself as well as for others?" and should I be able to say to myself, "Every one may make a deceitful promise when he finds himself in a difficulty from which he cannot otherwise extricate himself?" Then I presently become aware that while I can will the lie, I can by no means will that lying should be a universal law. For with such a law there would be no promises at all, since it would be in vain to allege my intention in regard to my future actions to those who would not believe this allegation, or if they over hastily did so would pay me back in my own coin. Hence my maxim, as soon as it should be made a universal law, would necessarily destroy itself.

I do not, therefore, need any far-reaching penetration to discern what I have to do in order that my will may be morally good. Inexperienced in the course of the world, incapable of being prepared for all its contingencies, I only ask myself: Canst thou also will that thy maxim should be a universal law? If not, then it must be rejected, and that not because of a disadvantage accruing from it to myself or even to others, but because it cannot enter as a principle into a possible universal legislation, and reason extorts from me immediate respect for such legislation. I do not indeed as yet discern on what this respect is based (this the philosopher may inquire), but at least I understand this, that it is an estimation of the worth which far outweighs all worth of what is recommended by inclination, and that the necessity of acting from pure respect for the practical law is what constitutes duty, to which every other motive must give place, because it is the condition of a will being good in itself, and the worth of such a will is above everything.

Thus, then, without quitting the moral knowledge of common human reason, we have arrived at its principle. And although, no doubt, common men do not conceive it in such an abstract and universal form, yet they always have it really before their eyes and use it as the standard of their decision. Here it would be easy to show how, with this compass in hand, men are well able to distinguish, in every case that occurs, what is good, what bad, conformably to duty or inconsistent with it, if, without in the least teaching them anything new, we only, like Socrates, direct their attention to the principle they themselves employ; and that, therefore, we do not need science and philosophy to know what we should do to be honest and good, yea, even wise and virtuous. Indeed we might well have conjectured beforehand that the knowledge of what every man is bound to do, and therefore also to know, would be within the reach of every man, even the commonest. Here we cannot forbear admiration when we see how great an advantage the practical judgement has over the theoretical in the common understanding of men. In the latter, if common reason ventures to depart from the laws of experience and from the perceptions of the senses, it falls into mere inconceivabilities and self-contradictions, at least into a chaos of uncertainty, obscurity, and instability. But in the practical sphere it is just when the common understanding excludes all sensible springs from practical laws that its power of judgement begins to show itself to advantage. It then becomes even subtle, whether it be that it chicanes with its own conscience or with other claims respecting what is to be called right, or whether it desires for its own instruction to determine honestly the worth of actions; and, in the latter case, it may even have as good a hope of hitting the mark as any philosopher whatever can promise himself. Nay, it is almost more sure of doing so, because the philosopher cannot have any other principle, while he may easily perplex his judgement by a multitude of considerations foreign to the matter, and so turn aside from the right way. Would it not therefore be wiser in moral concerns to acquiesce in the judgement of common reason, or at most only to call in philosophy for the purpose of rendering the system of morals more complete and intelligible, and its rules more convenient for use (especially for disputation), but not so as to draw off the common understanding from its happy simplicity, or to bring it by means of philosophy into a new path of inquiry and instruction?

Innocence is indeed a glorious thing; only, on the other hand, it is very sad that it cannot well maintain itself and is easily seduced. On this account even wisdom-which otherwise consists more in conduct than in knowledge- yet has need of science, not in order to learn from it, but to secure for its precepts admission and permanence. Against all the commands of duty which reason represents to man as so deserving of respect, he feels in himself a powerful counterpoise in his wants and inclinations, the entire satisfaction of which he sums up under the name of happiness. Now reason issues its commands unyieldingly, without promising anything to the inclinations, and, as it were, with disregard and contempt for these claims, which are so impetuous, and at the same time so plausible, and which will not allow themselves to be suppressed by any command. Hence there arises a natural dialectic, *i.e.*, a disposition, to argue against these strict laws of duty and to question their validity, or at least their purity and strictness; and, if possible, to make them more accordant with our wishes and inclinations, that is to say, to corrupt them at their very source, and entirely to destroy their worth- a thing which even common practical reason cannot ultimately call good.

Thus is the common reason of man compelled to go out of its sphere, and to take a step into the field of a practical philosophy, not to satisfy any speculative want (which never occurs to it as long as it is content to be mere sound reason), but even on practical grounds, in order to attain in it information and clear instruction respecting the source of its principle, and the correct determination of it in opposition to the maxims which are based on wants and inclinations, so that it may escape from the perplexity of opposite claims and not run the risk of losing all genuine moral principles through the equivocation into which it easily falls. Thus, when practical reason cultivates itself, there insensibly arises in it a dialetic which forces it to seek aid in philosophy, just as happens to it in its theoretic use; and in this case, therefore, as well as in the other, it will find rest nowhere but in a thorough critical examination of our reason.

Second Section

Transition From Popular Moral Philosophy
To The Metaphysic Of Morals

If we have hitherto drawn our notion of duty from the common use of our practical reason, it is by no means to be inferred that we have treated it as an empirical notion. On the contrary, if we attend to the experience of men's conduct, we meet frequent and, as we ourselves allow, just complaints that one cannot find a single certain example of the disposition to act from pure duty. Although many things are done in conformity with what duty prescribes, it is nevertheless always doubtful whether they are done strictly from duty, so as to have a moral worth. Hence there have at all times been philosophers who have altogether denied that this disposition actually exists at all in human actions, and have ascribed everything to a more or less refined self-love. Not that they have on that account questioned the soundness of the conception of morality; on the contrary, they spoke with sincere regret of the frailty and corruption of human nature, which, though noble enough to take its rule an idea so worthy of respect, is yet weak to follow it and employs reason which ought to give it the law only for the purpose of providing for the interest of the inclinations, whether singly or at the best in the greatest possible harmony with one another.

In fact, it is absolutely impossible to make out by experience with complete certainty a single case in which the maxim of an action, however right in itself, rested simply on moral grounds and on the conception of duty. Sometimes it happens that with the sharpest self-examination we can find nothing beside the moral principle of duty which could have been powerful enough to move us to this or that action and to so great a sacrifice; yet we cannot from this infer with certainty that it was not really some secret impulse of self-love, under the false appearance of duty, that was the actual determining cause of the will. We like them to flatter ourselves by falsely taking credit for a more noble motive; whereas in fact we can never, even by the strictest examination, get completely behind the secret springs of action; since, when the question is of moral worth, it is not with the actions which we see that we are concerned, but with those inward principles of them which we do not see.

Moreover, we cannot better serve the wishes of those who ridicule all morality as a mere chimera of human imagination over stepping itself from vanity, than by conceding to them that notions of duty must be drawn only from experience (as from indolence, people are ready to think is also the case with all other notions); for or is to prepare for them a certain triumph. I am willing to admit out of love of humanity that even most of our actions are correct, but if we look closer at them we everywhere come upon the dear self which is always prominent, and it is this they have in view and not the strict command of duty which would often require self-denial. Without being an enemy of virtue, a cool observer, one that does not mistake the wish for good, however lively, for its reality, may sometimes doubt whether true virtue is actually found anywhere in the world, and this especially as years increase and the judgement is partly made wiser by experience and partly, also, more acute in observation. This being so, nothing can secure us from falling away altogether from our ideas of duty, or maintain in the soul a well-grounded respect for its law, but the clear conviction that although there should never have been actions which really sprang from such pure sources, yet whether this or that takes place is not at all the question; but that reason of itself, independent on all experience, ordains what ought to take place, that accordingly actions of which perhaps the world has hitherto never given an example, the feasibility even of which might be very much doubted by one who founds everything on experience, are nevertheless inflexibly commanded by reason; that, e.g., even though there might never yet have been a sincere friend, yet not a whit the less is pure sincerity in friendship required of every man, because, prior to all experience, this duty is involved as duty in the idea of a reason determining the will by a priori principles.

When we add further that, unless we deny that the notion of morality has any truth or reference to any possible object, we must admit that its law must be valid, not merely for men but for all rational creatures generally, not merely under certain contingent conditions or with exceptions but with absolute necessity, then it is clear that no experience could enable us to infer even the possibility of such apodeictic laws. For with what right could we bring into unbounded respect as a universal precept for every rational nature that which perhaps holds only under the contingent conditions of humanity? Or how could laws of the determination of our will be regarded as laws of the determination of the will of rational beings generally, and for us only as such, if they were merely empirical and did not take their origin wholly a priori from pure but practical reason?

Nor could anything be more fatal to morality than that we should wish to derive it from examples. For every example of it that is set before me must be first itself tested by principles of morality, whether it is worthy to serve as an original example, i.e., as a pattern; but by no means can it authoritatively furnish the conception of morality. Even the Holy One of the Gospels must first be compared with our ideal of moral perfection before we can recognise Him as such; and so He says of Himself, "Why call ye Me (whom you see) good; none is good (the model of good) but God only (whom ye do not see)?" But whence have we the conception of God as the supreme good? Simply from the idea of moral perfection, which reason frames a priori and connects inseparably with the notion of a free will. Imitation finds no place at all in morality, and examples serve only for encouragement, i.e., they put beyond doubt the feasibility of what the law commands, they make visible that which the practical rule expresses more generally, but they can never authorize us to set aside the true original which lies in reason and to guide ourselves by examples.

If then there is no genuine supreme principle of morality but what must rest simply on pure reason, independent of all experience, I think it is not necessary even to put the question whether it is good to exhibit these concepts in their generality (in abstracto) as they are established a priori along with the principles belonging to them, if our knowledge is to be distinguished from the vulgar and to be called philosophical.

In our times indeed this might perhaps be necessary; for if we collected votes whether pure rational knowledge separated from everything empirical, that is to say, metaphysic of morals, or whether popular practical philosophy is to be preferred, it is easy to guess which side would preponderate.

This descending to popular notions is certainly very commendable, if the ascent to the principles of pure reason has first taken place and been satisfactorily accomplished. This implies that we first found ethics on metaphysics, and then, when it is firmly established, procure a hearing for it by giving it a popular character. But it is quite absurd to try to be popular in the first inquiry, on which the soundness of the principles depends. It is not only that this proceeding can never lay claim to the very rare merit of a true philosophical popularity, since there is no art in being intelligible if one renounces all thoroughness of insight; but also it produces a disgusting medley of compiled observations and half-reasoned principles. Shallow pates enjoy this because it can be used for every-day chat, but the sagacious find in it only confusion, and being unsatisfied and unable to help themselves, they turn away their eyes, while philosophers, who see quite well through this delusion, are little listened to when they call men off for a time from this pretended popularity, in order that they might be rightfully popular after they have attained a definite insight.

We need only look at the attempts of moralists in that favourite fashion, and we shall find at one time the special constitution of human nature (including, however, the idea of a rational nature generally), at one time perfection, at another happiness, here moral sense, there fear of God. a little of this, and a little of that, in marvellous mixture, without its occurring to them to ask whether the principles of morality are to be sought in the knowledge of human nature at all (which we can have only from experience); or, if this is not so, if these principles are to be found altogether a priori, free from everything empirical, in pure rational concepts only and nowhere else, not even in the smallest degree; then rather to adopt the method of making this a separate inquiry, as pure practical philosophy, or (if one may use a name so decried) as metaphysic of morals,[3] to bring it by itself to completeness, and to require the public, which wishes for popular treatment, to await the issue of this undertaking.

Such a metaphysic of morals, completely isolated, not mixed with any anthropology, theology, physics, or hyperphysics, and still less with occult qualities (which we might call hypophysical), is not only an indispensable substratum of all sound theoretical knowledge of duties, but is at the same time a desideratum of the highest importance to the actual fulfilment of their precepts. For the pure conception

---

[3] Just as pure mathematics are distinguished from applied, pure logic from applied, so if we choose we may also distinguish pure philosophy of morals (metaphysic) from applied (viz., applied to human nature). By this designation we are also at once reminded that moral principles are not based on properties of human nature, but must subsist a priori of themselves, while from such principles practical rules must be capable of being deduced for every rational nature, and accordingly for that of man.

of duty, unmixed with any foreign addition of empirical attractions, and, in a word, the conception of the moral law, exercises on the human heart, by way of reason alone (which first becomes aware with this that it can of itself be practical), an influence so much more powerful than all other springs[4] which may be derived from the field of experience, that, in the consciousness of its worth, it despises the latter, and can by degrees become their master; whereas a mixed ethics, compounded partly of motives drawn from feelings and inclinations, and partly also of conceptions of reason, must make the mind waver between motives which cannot be brought under any principle, which lead to good only by mere accident and very often also to evil.

From what has been said, it is clear that all moral conceptions have their seat and origin completely a priori in the reason, and that, moreover, in the commonest reason just as truly as in that which is in the highest degree speculative; that they cannot be obtained by abstraction from any empirical, and therefore merely contingent, knowledge; that it is just this purity of their origin that makes them worthy to serve as our supreme practical principle, and that just in proportion as we add anything empirical, we detract from their genuine influence and from the absolute value of actions; that it is not only of the greatest necessity, in a purely speculative point of view, but is also of the greatest practical importance, to derive these notions and laws from pure reason, to present them pure and unmixed, and even to determine the compass of this practical or pure rational knowledge, *i.e.*, to determine the whole faculty of pure practical reason; and, in doing so, we must not make its principles dependent on the particular nature of human reason, though in speculative philosophy this may be permitted, or may even at times be necessary; but since moral laws ought to hold good for every rational creature, we must derive them from the general concept of a rational being. In this way, although for its application to man morality has need of anthropology, yet, in the first instance, we must treat it independently as pure philosophy, *i.e.*, as metaphysic, complete in itself (a thing which in such distinct branches of science is easily done); knowing well that unless we are in possession of this, it would not only be vain to determine the moral element of duty

---

[4] I have a letter from the late excellent Sulzer, in which he asks me what can be the reason that moral instruction, although containing much that is convincing for the reason, yet accomplishes so little? My answer was postponed in order that I might make it complete. But it is simply this: that the teachers themselves have not got their own notions clear, and when they endeavour to make up for this by raking up motives of moral goodness from every quarter, trying to make their physic right strong, they spoil it. For the commonest understanding shows that if we imagine, on the one hand, an act of honesty done with steadfast mind, apart from every view to advantage of any kind in this world or another, and even under the greatest temptations of necessity or allurement, and, on the other hand, a similar act which was affected, in however low a degree, by a foreign motive, the former leaves far behind and eclipses the second; it elevates the soul and inspires the wish to be able to act in like manner oneself. Even moderately young children feel this impression, ana one should never represent duties to them in any other light.

in right actions for purposes of speculative criticism, but it would be impossible to base morals on their genuine principles, even for common practical purposes, especially of moral instruction, so as to produce pure moral dispositions, and to engraft them on men's minds to the promotion of the greatest possible good in the world.

But in order that in this study we may not merely advance by the natural steps from the common moral judgement (in this case very worthy of respect) to the philosophical, as has been already done, but also from a popular philosophy, which goes no further than it can reach by groping with the help of examples, to metaphysic (which does allow itself to be checked by anything empirical and, as it must measure the whole extent of this kind of rational knowledge, goes as far as ideal conceptions, where even examples fail us), we must follow and clearly describe the practical faculty of reason, from the general rules of its determination to the point where the notion of duty springs from it.

Everything in nature works according to laws. Rational beings alone have the faculty of acting according to the conception of laws, that is according to principles, *i.e.*, have a will. Since the deduction of actions from principles requires reason, the will is nothing but practical reason. If reason infallibly determines the will, then the actions of such a being which are recognised as objectively necessary are subjectively necessary also, *i.e.*, the will is a faculty to choose that only which reason independent of inclination recognises as practically necessary, *i.e.*, as good. But if reason of itself does not sufficiently determine the will, if the latter is subject also to subjective conditions (particular impulses) which do not always coincide with the objective conditions; in a word, if the will does not in itself completely accord with reason (which is actually the case with men), then the actions which objectively are recognised as necessary are subjectively contingent, and the determination of such a will according to objective laws is obligation, that is to say, the relation of the objective laws to a will that is not thoroughly good is conceived as the determination of the will of a rational being by principles of reason, but which the will from its nature does not of necessity follow.

The conception of an objective principle, in so far as it is obligatory for a will, is called a command (of reason), and the formula of the command is called an imperative.

All imperatives are expressed by the word ought [or shall], and thereby indicate the relation of an objective law of reason to a will, which from its subjective constitution is not necessarily determined by it (an obligation). They say that something would be good to do or to forbear, but they say it to a will which does not always do a thing because it is conceived to be good to do it. That is practically good, however, which determines the will by means of the conceptions of reason, and consequently not from subjective causes, but objectively, that is on principles which are valid for every rational being as such. It is distinguished from the pleasant, as that which influences the will only by means of sensation from merely subjective causes, valid only for the sense of this or that one, and not as a principle of reason, which holds for every one.[5]

A perfectly good will would therefore be equally subject to objective laws (viz., laws of good), but could not be conceived as obliged thereby to act lawfully, because of itself from its subjective constitution it can only be determined by the conception of good. Therefore no imperatives hold for the Divine will, or in general for a holy will; ought is here out of place, because the volition is already of itself necessarily in unison with the law. Therefore imperatives are only formulae to express the relation of objective laws of all volition to the subjective imperfection of the will of this or that rational being, e.g., the human will.

Now all imperatives command either hypothetically or categorically. The former represent the practical necessity of a possible action as means to something else that is willed (or at least which one might possibly will). The categorical imperative would be that which represented an action as necessary of itself without reference to another end, *i.e.*, as objectively necessary.

Since every practical law represents a possible action as good and, on this account, for a subject who is practically determinable by reason, necessary, all imperatives are formulae determining an action which is necessary according to the principle of a will good in some respects. If now the action is good only as a means to something else, then the imperative is hypothetical; if it is conceived as good in itself and consequently as being necessarily the principle of a will which of itself conforms to reason, then it is categorical.

Thus the imperative declares what action possible by me would be good and presents the practical rule in relation to a will which does not forthwith perform an action simply because it is good, whether because the subject does not always know that it is good, or because, even if it know this, yet its maxims might be opposed to the objective principles of practical reason.

Accordingly the hypothetical imperative only says that the action is good for some purpose, possible or actual. In the first case it is a problematical, in the second

---

[5] The dependence of the desires on sensations is called inclination, and this accordingly always indicates a want. The dependence of a contingently determinable will on principles of reason is called an interest. This therefore, is found only in the case of a dependent will which does not always of itself conform to reason; in the Divine will we cannot conceive any interest. But the human will can also take an interest in a thing without therefore acting from interest. The former signifies the practical interest in the action, the latter the pathological in the object of the action. The former indicates only dependence of the will on principles of reason in themselves; the second, dependence on principles of reason for the sake of inclination, reason supplying only the practical rules how the requirement of the inclination may be satisfied. In the first case the action interests me; in the second the object of the action (because it is pleasant to me). We have seen in the first section that in an action done from duty we must look not to the interest in the object, but only to that in the action itself, and in its rational principle (viz., the law).

an assertorial practical principle. The categorical imperative which declares an action to be objectively necessary in itself without reference to any purpose, *i.e.*, without any other end, is valid as an apodeictic (practical) principle.

Whatever is possible only by the power of some rational being may also be conceived as a possible purpose of some will; and therefore the principles of action as regards the means necessary to attain some possible purpose are in fact infinitely numerous. All sciences have a practical part, consisting of problems expressing that some end is possible for us and of imperatives directing how it may be attained. These may, therefore, be called in general imperatives of skill. Here there is no question whether the end is rational and good, but only what one must do in order to attain it. The precepts for the physician to make his patient thoroughly healthy, and for a poisoner to ensure certain death, are of equal value in this respect, that each serves to effect its purpose perfectly. Since in early youth it cannot be known what ends are likely to occur to us in the course of life, parents seek to have their children taught a great many things, and provide for their skill in the use of means for all sorts of arbitrary ends, of none of which can they determine whether it may not perhaps hereafter be an object to their pupil, but which it is at all events possible that he might aim at; and this anxiety is so great that they commonly neglect to form and correct their judgement on the value of the things which may be chosen as ends.

There is one end, however, which may be assumed to be actually such to all rational beings (so far as imperatives apply to them, viz., as dependent beings), and, therefore, one purpose which they not merely may have, but which we may with certainty assume that they all actually have by a natural necessity, and this is happiness. The hypothetical imperative which expresses the practical necessity of an action as means to the advancement of happiness is assertorial. We are not to present it as necessary for an uncertain and merely possible purpose, but for a purpose which we may presuppose with certainty and a priori in every man, because it belongs to his being. Now skill in the choice of means to his own greatest well-being may be called prudence,[6] in the narrowest sense. And thus the imperative which refers to the choice of means to one's own happiness, *i.e.*, the precept of prudence, is still always hypothetical; the action is not commanded absolutely, but only as means to another purpose.

Finally, there is an imperative which commands a certain conduct immediately, without having as its condition any other purpose to be attained by it. This imperative is categorical. It concerns not the matter of the action, or its intended result, but its form and the principle of which it is itself a result; and what is essentially good in it

---

[6] The word prudence is taken in two senses: in the one it may bear the name of knowledge of the world, in the other that of private prudence. The former is a man's ability to influence others so as to use them for his own purposes. The latter is the sagacity to combine all these purposes for his own lasting benefit. This latter is properly that to which the value even of the former is reduced, and when a man is prudent in the former sense, but not in the latter, we might better say of him that he is clever and cunning, but, on the whole, imprudent.

consists in the mental disposition, let the consequence be what it may. This imperative may be called that of morality.

There is a marked distinction also between the volitions on these three sorts of principles in the dissimilarity of the obligation of the will. In order to mark this difference more clearly, I think they would be most suitably named in their order if we said they are either rules of skill, or counsels of prudence, or commands (laws) of morality. For it is law only that involves the conception of an unconditional and objective necessity, which is consequently universally valid; and commands are laws which must be obeyed, that is, must be followed, even in opposition to inclination. Counsels, indeed, involve necessity, but one which can only hold under a contingent subjective condition, viz., they depend on whether this or that man reckons this or that as part of his happiness; the categorical imperative, on the contrary, is not limited by any condition, and as being absolutely, although practically, necessary, may be quite properly called a command. We might also call the first kind of imperatives technical (belonging to art), the second pragmatic[7] (to welfare), the third moral (belonging to free conduct generally, that is, to morals).

Now arises the question, how are all these imperatives possible? This question does not seek to know how we can conceive the accomplishment of the action which the imperative ordains, but merely how we can conceive the obligation of the will which the imperative expresses. No special explanation is needed to show how an imperative of skill is possible. Whoever wills the end, wills also (so far as reason decides his conduct) the means in his power which are indispensably necessary thereto. This proposition is, as regards the volition, analytical; for, in willing an object as my effect, there is already thought the causality of myself as an acting cause, that is to say, the use of the means; and the imperative educes from the conception of volition of an end the conception of actions necessary to this end. Synthetical propositions must no doubt be employed in defining the means to a proposed end; but they do not concern the principle, the act of the will, but the object and its realization. E.g., that in order to bisect a line on an unerring principle I must draw from its extremities two intersecting arcs; this no doubt is taught by mathematics only in synthetical propositions; but if I know that it is only by this process that the intended operation can be performed, then to say that, if I fully will the operation, I also will the action required for it, is an analytical proposition; for it is one and the same thing to conceive something as an effect which I can produce in a certain way, and to conceive myself as acting in this way.

If it were only equally easy to give a definite conception of happiness, the imperatives of prudence would correspond exactly with those of skill, and would

---

[7] It seems to me that the proper signification of the word pragmatic may be most accurately defined in this way. For sanctions are called pragmatic which flow properly not from the law of the states as necessary enactments, but from precaution for the general welfare. A history is composed pragmatically when it teaches prudence, *i.e.*, instructs the world how it can provide for its interests better, or at least as well as, the men of former time.

likewise be analytical. For in this case as in that, it could be said: "Whoever wills the end, wills also (according to the dictate of reason necessarily) the indispensable means thereto which are in his power." But, unfortunately, the notion of happiness is so indefinite that although every man wishes to attain it, yet he never can say definitely and consistently what it is that he really wishes and wills. The reason of this is that all the elements which belong to the notion of happiness are altogether empirical, *i.e.*, they must be borrowed from experience, and nevertheless the idea of happiness requires an absolute whole, a maximum of welfare in my present and all future circumstances. Now it is impossible that the most clear-sighted and at the same time most powerful being (supposed finite) should frame to himself a definite conception of what he really wills in this. Does he will riches, how much anxiety, envy, and snares might he not thereby draw upon his shoulders? Does he will knowledge and discernment, perhaps it might prove to be only an eye so much the sharper to show him so much the more fearfully the evils that are now concealed from him, and that cannot be avoided, or to impose more wants on his desires, which already give him concern enough. Would he have long life? who guarantees to him that it would not be a long misery? would he at least have health? how often has uneasiness of the body restrained from excesses into which perfect health would have allowed one to fall? and so on. In short, he is unable, on any principle, to determine with certainty what would make him truly happy; because to do so he would need to be omniscient. We cannot therefore act on any definite principles to secure happiness, but only on empirical counsels, e.g. of regimen, frugality, courtesy, reserve, etc., which experience teaches do, on the average, most promote well-being. Hence it follows that the imperatives of prudence do not, strictly speaking, command at all, that is, they cannot present actions objectively as practically necessary; that they are rather to be regarded as counsels (consilia) than precepts precepts of reason, that the problem to determine certainly and universally what action would promote the happiness of a rational being is completely insoluble, and consequently no imperative respecting it is possible which should, in the strict sense, command to do what makes happy; because happiness is not an ideal of reason but of imagination, resting solely on empirical grounds, and it is vain to expect that these should define an action by which one could attain the totality of a series of consequences which is really endless. This imperative of prudence would however be an analytical proposition if we assume that the means to happiness could be certainly assigned; for it is distinguished from the imperative of skill only by this, that in the latter the end is merely possible, in the former it is given; as however both only ordain the means to that which we suppose to be willed as an end, it follows that the imperative which ordains the willing of the means to him who wills the end is in both cases analytical. Thus there is no difficulty in regard to the possibility of an imperative of this kind either.

On the other hand, the question how the imperative of morality is possible, is undoubtedly one, the only one, demanding a solution, as this is not at all hypothetical, and the objective necessity which it presents cannot rest on any hypothesis, as is the case with the hypothetical imperatives. Only here we must never leave out of consideration that we cannot make out by any example, in other words empirically, whether there is such an imperative at all, but it is rather to be feared that all those which seem to be categorical may yet be at bottom hypothetical. For instance, when the precept is: "Thou shalt not promise deceitfully"; and it is assumed that the necessity of this is not a mere counsel to avoid some other evil, so that it should mean: "Thou shalt not make a lying promise, lest if it become known thou shouldst destroy thy credit," but that an action of this kind must be regarded as evil in itself, so that the imperative of the prohibition is categorical; then we cannot show with certainty in any example that the will was determined merely by the law, without any other spring of action, although it may appear to be so. For it is always possible that fear of disgrace, perhaps also obscure dread of other dangers, may have a secret influence on the will. Who can prove by experience the non-existence of a cause when all that experience tells us is that we do not perceive it? But in such a case the so-called moral imperative, which as such appears to be categorical and unconditional, would in reality be only a pragmatic precept, drawing our attention to our own interests and merely teaching us to take these into consideration.

We shall therefore have to investigate a priori the possibility of a categorical imperative, as we have not in this case the advantage of its reality being given in experience, so that [the elucidation of] its possibility should be requisite only for its explanation, not for its establishment. In the meantime it may be discerned beforehand that the categorical imperative alone has the purport of a practical law; all the rest may indeed be called principles of the will but not laws, since whatever is only necessary for the attainment of some arbitrary purpose may be considered as in itself contingent, and we can at any time be free from the precept if we give up the purpose; on the contrary, the unconditional command leaves the will no liberty to choose the opposite; consequently it alone carries with it that necessity which we require in a law.

Secondly, in the case of this categorical imperative or law of morality, the difficulty (of discerning its possibility) is a very profound one. It is an a priori synthetical practical proposition;[8] and as there is so much difficulty in discerning the possibility of speculative propositions of this kind, it may readily be supposed that the difficulty will be no less with the practical.

In this problem we will first inquire whether the mere conception of a categorical imperative may not perhaps supply us also with the formula of it, containing the proposition which alone can be a categorical imperative; for even if we know the tenor of such an absolute command, yet how it is possible will require further special and laborious study, which we postpone to the last section.

---

[8] I connect the act with the will without presupposing any condition resulting from any inclination, but a priori, and therefore necessarily (though only objectively, i.e., assuming the idea of a reason possessing full power over all subjective motives). This is accordingly a practical proposition which does not deduce the willing of an action by mere analysis from another already presupposed (for we have not such a perfect will), but connects it immediately with the conception of the will of a rational being, as something not contained in it.

When I conceive a hypothetical imperative, in general I do not know beforehand what it will contain until I am given the condition. But when I conceive a categorical imperative, I know at once what it contains. For as the imperative contains besides the law only the necessity that the maxims[9] shall conform to this law, while the law contains no conditions restricting it, there remains nothing but the general statement that the maxim of the action should conform to a universal law, and it is this conformity alone that the imperative properly represents as necessary.

There is therefore but one categorical imperative, namely, this: Act only on that maxim whereby thou canst at the same time will that it should become a universal law.

Now if all imperatives of duty can be deduced from this one imperative as from their principle, then, although it should remain undecided what is called duty is not merely a vain notion, yet at least we shall be able to show what we understand by it and what this notion means.

Since the universality of the law according to which effects are produced constitutes what is properly called nature in the most general sense (as to form), that is the existence of things so far as it is determined by general laws, the imperative of duty may be expressed thus: Act as if the maxim of thy action were to become by thy will a universal law of nature.

We will now enumerate a few duties, adopting the usual division of them into duties to ourselves and ourselves and to others, and into perfect and imperfect duties.[10]

1. A man reduced to despair by a series of misfortunes feels wearied of life, but is still so far in possession of his reason that he can ask himself whether it would not be contrary to his duty to himself to take his own life. Now he inquires whether the maxim of his action could become a universal law of nature. His maxim is: "From self-love I adopt it as a principle to shorten my life when its longer duration is likely to bring more evil than satisfaction." It is asked then simply whether this principle founded on self-love can become a universal law of nature. Now we see at once that a system of nature of which it should be a law to destroy life by means of the very feeling whose special nature it is to impel to the improvement of life would contradict

---

[9] A maxim is a subjective principle of action, and must be distinguished from the objective principle, namely, practical law. The former contains the practical rule set by reason according to the conditions of the subject (often its ignorance or its inclinations), so that it is the principle on which the subject acts; but the law is the objective principle valid for every rational being, and is the principle on which it ought to act that is an imperative.

[10] It must be noted here that I reserve the division of duties for a future metaphysic of morals; so that I give it here only as an arbitrary one (in order to arrange my examples). For the rest, I understand by a perfect duty one that admits no exception in favour of inclination and then I have not merely external but also internal perfect duties. This is contrary to the use of the word adopted in the schools; but I do not intend to justify there, as it is all one for my purpose whether it is admitted or not.

itself and, therefore, could not exist as a system of nature; hence that maxim cannot possibly exist as a universal law of nature and, consequently, would be wholly inconsistent with the supreme principle of all duty.

2. Another finds himself forced by necessity to borrow money. He knows that he will not be able to repay it, but sees also that nothing will be lent to him unless he promises stoutly to repay it in a definite time. He desires to make this promise, but he has still so much conscience as to ask himself: "Is it not unlawful and inconsistent with duty to get out of a difficulty in this way?" Suppose however that he resolves to do so: then the maxim of his action would be expressed thus: "When I think myself in want of money, I will borrow money and promise to repay it, although I know that I never can do so." Now this principle of self-love or of one's own advantage may perhaps be consistent with my whole future welfare; but the question now is, "Is it right?" I change then the suggestion of self-love into a universal law, and state the question thus: "How would it be if my maxim were a universal law?" Then I see at once that it could never hold as a universal law of nature, but would necessarily contradict itself. For supposing it to be a universal law that everyone when he thinks himself in a difficulty should be able to promise whatever he pleases, with the purpose of not keeping his promise, the promise itself would become impossible, as well as the end that one might have in view in it, since no one would consider that anything was promised to him, but would ridicule all such statements as vain pretences.

3. A third finds in himself a talent which with the help of some culture might make him a useful man in many respects. But he finds himself in comfortable circumstances and prefers to indulge in pleasure rather than to take pains in enlarging and improving his happy natural capacities. He asks, however, whether his maxim of neglect of his natural gifts, besides agreeing with his inclination to indulgence, agrees also with what is called duty. He sees then that a system of nature could indeed subsist with such a universal law although men (like the South Sea islanders) should let their talents rest and resolve to devote their lives merely to idleness, amusement, and propagation of their species- in a word, to enjoyment; but he cannot possibly will that this should be a universal law of nature, or be implanted in us as such by a natural instinct. For, as a rational being, he necessarily wills that his faculties be developed, since they serve him and have been given him, for all sorts of possible purposes.

4. A fourth, who is in prosperity, while he sees that others have to contend with great wretchedness and that he could help them, thinks: "What concern is it of mine? Let everyone be as happy as Heaven pleases, or as he can make himself; I will take nothing from him nor even envy him, only I do not wish to contribute anything to his welfare or to his assistance in distress!" Now no doubt if such a mode of thinking were a universal law, the human race might very well subsist and doubtless even better than in a state in which everyone talks of sympathy and good-will, or even takes care occasionally to put it into practice, but, on the other side, also cheats when he can, betrays the rights of men, or otherwise violates them. But although it is possible that a universal law of nature might exist in accordance with that maxim, it is

impossible to will that such a principle should have the universal validity of a law of nature. For a will which resolved this would contradict itself, inasmuch as many cases might occur in which one would have need of the love and sympathy of others, and in which, by such a law of nature, sprung from his own will, he would deprive himself of all hope of the aid he desires.

These are a few of the many actual duties, or at least what we regard as such, which obviously fall into two classes on the one principle that we have laid down. We must be able to will that a maxim of our action should be a universal law. This is the canon of the moral appreciation of the action generally. Some actions are of such a character that their maxim cannot without contradiction be even conceived as a universal law of nature, far from it being possible that we should will that it should be so. In others this intrinsic impossibility is not found, but still it is impossible to will that their maxim should be raised to the universality of a law of nature, since such a will would contradict itself It is easily seen that the former violate strict or rigorous (inflexible) duty; the latter only laxer (meritorious) duty. Thus it has been completely shown how all duties depend as regards the nature of the obligation (not the object of the action) on the same principle.

If now we attend to ourselves on occasion of any transgression of duty, we shall find that we in fact do not will that our maxim should be a universal law, for that is impossible for us; on the contrary, we will that the opposite should remain a universal law, only we assume the liberty of making an exception in our own favour or (just for this time only) in favour of our inclination. Consequently if we considered all cases from one and the same point of view, namely, that of reason, we should find a contradiction in our own will, namely, that a certain principle should be objectively necessary as a universal law, and yet subjectively should not be universal, but admit of exceptions. As however we at one moment regard our action from the point of view of a will wholly conformed to reason, and then again look at the same action from the point of view of a will affected by inclination, there is not really any contradiction, but an antagonism of inclination to the precept of reason, whereby the universality of the principle is changed into a mere generality, so that the practical principle of reason shall meet the maxim half way. Now, although this cannot be justified in our own impartial judgement, yet it proves that we do really recognise the validity of the categorical imperative and (with all respect for it) only allow ourselves a few exceptions, which we think unimportant and forced from us.

We have thus established at least this much, that if duty is a conception which is to have any import and real legislative authority for our actions, it can only be expressed in categorical and not at all in hypothetical imperatives. We have also, which is of great importance, exhibited clearly and definitely for every practical application the content of the categorical imperative, which must contain the principle of all duty if there is such a thing at all. We have not yet, however, advanced so far as to prove a priori that there actually is such an imperative, that there is a practical law which commands absolutely of itself and without any other impulse, and that the following of this law is duty.

With the view of attaining to this, it is of extreme importance to remember that we must not allow ourselves to think of deducing the reality of this principle from the particular attributes of human nature. For duty is to be a practical, unconditional necessity of action; it must therefore hold for all rational beings (to whom an imperative can apply at all), and for this reason only be also a law for all human wills. On the contrary, whatever is deduced from the particular natural characteristics of humanity, from certain feelings and propensions, nay, even, if possible, from any particular tendency proper to human reason, and which need not necessarily hold for the will of every rational being; this may indeed supply us with a maxim, but not with a law; with a subjective principle on which we may have a propension and inclination to act, but not with an objective principle on which we should be enjoined to act, even though all our propensions, inclinations, and natural dispositions were opposed to it. In fact, the sublimity and intrinsic dignity of the command in duty are so much the more evident, the less the subjective impulses favour it and the more they oppose it, without being able in the slightest degree to weaken the obligation of the law or to diminish its validity.

Here then we see philosophy brought to a critical position, since it has to be firmly fixed, notwithstanding that it has nothing to support it in heaven or earth. Here it must show its purity as absolute director of its own laws, not the herald of those which are whispered to it by an implanted sense or who knows what tutelary nature. Although these may be better than nothing, yet they can never afford principles dictated by reason, which must have their source wholly a priori and thence their commanding authority, expecting everything from the supremacy of the law and the due respect for it, nothing from inclination, or else condemning the man to self-contempt and inward abhorrence.

Thus every empirical element is not only quite incapable of being an aid to the principle of morality, but is even highly prejudicial to the purity of morals, for the proper and inestimable worth of an absolutely good will consists just in this, that the principle of action is free from all influence of contingent grounds, which alone experience can furnish. We cannot too much or too often repeat our warning against this lax and even mean habit of thought which seeks for its principle amongst empirical motives and laws; for human reason in its weariness is glad to rest on this pillow, and in a dream of sweet illusions (in which, instead of Juno, it embraces a cloud) it substitutes for morality a bastard patched up from limbs of various derivation, which looks like anything one chooses to see in it, only not like virtue to one who has once beheld her in her true form.[11]

The question then is this: "Is it a necessary law for all rational beings that they should always judge of their actions by maxims of which they can themselves will that

---

[11] To behold virtue in her proper form is nothing else but to contemplate morality stripped of all admixture of sensible things and of every spurious ornament of reward or self-love. How much she then eclipses everything else that appears charming to the affections, every one may readily perceive with the least exertion of his reason, if it be not wholly spoiled for abstraction.

they should serve as universal laws?" If it is so, then it must be connected (altogether a priori) with the very conception of the will of a rational being generally. But in order to discover this connexion we must, however reluctantly, take a step into metaphysic, although into a domain of it which is distinct from speculative philosophy, namely, the metaphysic of morals. In a practical philosophy, where it is not the reasons of what happens that we have to ascertain, but the laws of what ought to happen, even although it never does, i.e., objective practical laws, there it is not necessary to inquire into the reasons why anything pleases or displeases, how the pleasure of mere sensation differs from taste, and whether the latter is distinct from a general satisfaction of reason; on what the feeling of pleasure or pain rests, and how from it desires and inclinations arise, and from these again maxims by the co-operation of reason: for all this belongs to an empirical psychology, which would constitute the second part of physics, if we regard physics as the philosophy of nature, so far as it is based on empirical laws. But here we are concerned with objective practical laws and, consequently, with the relation of the will to itself so far as it is determined by reason alone, in which case whatever has reference to anything empirical is necessarily excluded; since if reason of itself alone determines the conduct (and it is the possibility of this that we are now investigating), it must necessarily do so a priori.

The will is conceived as a faculty of determining oneself to action in accordance with the conception of certain laws. And such a faculty can be found only in rational beings. Now that which serves the will as the objective ground of its self-determination is the end, and, if this is assigned by reason alone, it must hold for all rational beings. On the other hand, that which merely contains the ground of possibility of the action of which the effect is the end, this is called the means. The subjective ground of the desire is the spring, the objective ground of the volition is the motive; hence the distinction between subjective ends which rest on springs, and objective ends which depend on motives valid for every rational being. Practical principles are formal when they abstract from all subjective ends; they are material when they assume these, and therefore particular springs of action. The ends which a rational being proposes to himself at pleasure as effects of his actions (material ends) are all only relative, for it is only their relation to the particular desires of the subject that gives them their worth, which therefore cannot furnish principles universal and necessary for all rational beings and for every volition, that is to say practical laws. Hence all these relative ends can give rise only to hypothetical imperatives.

Supposing, however, that there were something whose existence has in itself an absolute worth, something which, being an end in itself, could be a source of definite laws; then in this and this alone would lie the source of a possible categorical imperative, i.e., a practical law.

Now I say: man and generally any rational being exists as an end in himself, not merely as a means to be arbitrarily used by this or that will, but in all his actions, whether they concern himself or other rational beings, must be always regarded at the same time as an end. All objects of the inclinations have only a conditional worth, for if the inclinations and the wants founded on them did not exist, then their object would be without value. But the inclinations, themselves being sources of want, are so far from having an absolute worth for which they should be desired that on the contrary it must be the universal wish of every rational being to be wholly free from them. Thus the worth of any object which is to be acquired by our action is always conditional. Beings whose existence depends not on our will but on nature's, have nevertheless, if they are irrational beings, only a relative value as means, and are therefore called things; rational beings, on the contrary, are called persons, because their very nature points them out as ends in themselves, that is as something which must not be used merely as means, and so far therefore restricts freedom of action (and is an object of respect). These, therefore, are not merely subjective ends whose existence has a worth for us as an effect of our action, but objective ends, that is, things whose existence is an end in itself; an end moreover for which no other can be substituted, which they should subserve merely as means, for otherwise nothing whatever would possess absolute worth; but if all worth were conditioned and therefore contingent, then there would be no supreme practical principle of reason whatever.

If then there is a supreme practical principle or, in respect of the human will, a categorical imperative, it must be one which, being drawn from the conception of that which is necessarily an end for everyone because it is an end in itself, constitutes an objective principle of will, and can therefore serve as a universal practical law. The foundation of this principle is: rational nature exists as an end in itself. Man necessarily conceives his own existence as being so; so far then this is a subjective principle of human actions. But every other rational being regards its existence similarly, just on the same rational principle that holds for me:[12] so that it is at the same time an objective principle, from which as a supreme practical law all laws of the will must be capable of being deduced. Accordingly the practical imperative will be as follows: So act as to treat humanity, whether in thine own person or in that of any other, in every case as an end withal, never as means only. We will now inquire whether this can be practically carried out.

To abide by the previous examples:

Firstly, under the head of necessary duty to oneself: He who contemplates suicide should ask himself whether his action can be consistent with the idea of humanity as an end in itself. If he destroys himself in order to escape from painful circumstances, he uses a person merely as a mean to maintain a tolerable condition up to the end of life. But a man is not a thing, that is to say, something which can be used merely as means, but must in all his actions be always considered as an end in himself. I cannot, therefore, dispose in any way of a man in my own person so as to mutilate him, to damage or kill him. (It belongs to ethics proper to define this principle more precisely, so as to avoid all misunderstanding, e. g., as to the amputation of the limbs in order to preserve myself, as to exposing my life to danger with a view to preserve it, etc. This question is therefore omitted here.)

---

[12] This proposition is here stated as a postulate. The ground of it will be found in the concluding section.

Secondly, as regards necessary duties, or those of strict obligation, towards others: He who is thinking of making a lying promise to others will see at once that he would be using another man merely as a mean, without the latter containing at the same time the end in himself. For he whom I propose by such a promise to use for my own purposes cannot possibly assent to my mode of acting towards him and, therefore, cannot himself contain the end of this action. This violation of the principle of humanity in other men is more obvious if we take in examples of attacks on the freedom and property of others. For then it is clear that he who transgresses the rights of men intends to use the person of others merely as a means, without considering that as rational beings they ought always to be esteemed also as ends, that is, as beings who must be capable of containing in themselves the end of the very same action.[13]

Thirdly, as regards contingent (meritorious) duties to oneself: It is not enough that the action does not violate humanity in our own person as an end in itself, it must also harmonize with it. Now there are in humanity capacities of greater perfection, which belong to the end that nature has in view in regard to humanity in ourselves as the subject: to neglect these might perhaps be consistent with the maintenance of humanity as an end in itself, but not with the advancement of this end.

Fourthly, as regards meritorious duties towards others: The natural end which all men have is their own happiness. Now humanity might indeed subsist, although no one should contribute anything to the happiness of others, provided he did not intentionally withdraw anything from it; but after all this would only harmonize negatively not positively with humanity as an end in itself, if every one does not also endeavour, as far as in him lies, to forward the ends of others. For the ends of any subject which is an end in himself ought as far as possible to be my ends also, if that conception is to have its full effect with me.

This principle, that humanity and generally every rational nature is an end in itself (which is the supreme limiting condition of every man's freedom of action), is not borrowed from experience, firstly, because it is universal, applying as it does to all rational beings whatever, and experience is not capable of determining anything about them; secondly, because it does not present humanity as an end to men (subjectively), that is as an object which men do of themselves actually adopt as an end; but as an objective end, which must as a law constitute the supreme limiting condition of all our subjective ends, let them be what we will; it must therefore spring

---

[13] Let it not be thought that the common "quod tibi non vis fieri, etc." could serve here as the rule or principle. For it is only a deduction from the former, though with several limitations; it cannot be a universal law, for it does not contain the principle of duties to oneself, nor of the duties of benevolence to others (for many a one would gladly consent that others should not benefit him, provided only that he might be excused from showing benevolence to them), nor finally that of duties of strict obligation to one another, for on this principle the criminal might argue against the judge who punishes him, and so on.

from pure reason. In fact the objective principle of all practical legislation lies (according to the first principle) in the rule and its form of universality which makes it capable of being a law (say, e. g., a law of nature); but the subjective principle is in the end; now by the second principle the subject of all ends is each rational being, inasmuch as it is an end in itself. Hence follows the third practical principle of the will, which is the ultimate condition of its harmony with universal practical reason, viz.: the idea of the will of every rational being as a universally legislative will.

On this principle all maxims are rejected which are inconsistent with the will being itself universal legislator. Thus the will is not subject simply to the law, but so subject that it must be regarded as itself giving the law and, on this ground only, subject to the law (of which it can regard itself as the author).

In the previous imperatives, namely, that based on the conception of the conformity of actions to general laws, as in a physical system of nature, and that based on the universal prerogative of rational beings as ends in themselves- these imperatives, just because they were conceived as categorical, excluded from any share in their authority all admixture of any interest as a spring of action; they were, however, only assumed to be categorical, because such an assumption was necessary to explain the conception of duty. But we could not prove independently that there are practical propositions which command categorically, nor can it be proved in this section; one thing, however, could be done, namely, to indicate in the imperative itself, by some determinate expression, that in the case of volition from duty all interest is renounced, which is the specific criterion of categorical as distinguished from hypothetical imperatives. This is done in the present (third) formula of the principle, namely, in the idea of the will of every rational being as a universally legislating will.

For although a will which is subject to laws may be attached to this law by means of an interest, yet a will which is itself a supreme lawgiver so far as it is such cannot possibly depend on any interest, since a will so dependent would itself still need another law restricting the interest of its self-love by the condition that it should be valid as universal law.

Thus the principle that every human will is a will which in all its maxims gives universal laws,[14] provided it be otherwise justified, would be very well adapted to be the categorical imperative, in this respect, namely, that just because of the idea of universal legislation it is not based on interest, and therefore it alone among all possible imperatives can be unconditional. Or still better, converting the proposition, if there is a categorical imperative (*i.e.*, a law for the will of every rational being), it can only command that everything be done from maxims of one's will regarded as a will which could at the same time will that it should itself give universal laws, for in that case only the practical principle and the imperative which it obeys are unconditional, since they cannot be based on any interest.

---

[14] I may be excused from adducing examples to elucidate this principle, as those which have already been used to elucidate the categorical imperative and its formula would all serve for the like purpose here.

Looking back now on all previous attempts to discover the principle of morality, we need not wonder why they all failed. It was seen that man was bound to laws by duty, but it was not observed that the laws to which he is subject are only those of his own giving, though at the same time they are universal, and that he is only bound to act in conformity with his own will; a will, however, which is designed by nature to give universal laws. For when one has conceived man only as subject to a law (no matter what), then this law required some interest, either by way of attraction or constraint, since it did not originate as a law from his own will, but this will was according to a law obliged by something else to act in a certain manner. Now by this necessary consequence all the labour spent in finding a supreme principle of duty was irrevocably lost. For men never elicited duty, but only a necessity of acting from a certain interest. Whether this interest was private or otherwise, in any case the imperative must be conditional and could not by any means be capable of being a moral command. I will therefore call this the principle of autonomy of the will, in contrast with every other which I accordingly reckon as heteronomy.

The conception of the will of every rational being as one which must consider itself as giving in all the maxims of its will universal laws, so as to judge itself and its actions from this point of view- this conception leads to another which depends on it and is very fruitful, namely that of a kingdom of ends.

By a kingdom I understand the union of different rational beings in a system by common laws. Now since it is by laws that ends are determined as regards their universal validity, hence, if we abstract from the personal differences of rational beings and likewise from all the content of their private ends, we shall be able to conceive all ends combined in a systematic whole (including both rational beings as ends in themselves, and also the special ends which each may propose to himself), that is to say, we can conceive a kingdom of ends, which on the preceding principles is possible.

For all rational beings come under the law that each of them must treat itself and all others never merely as means, but in every case at the same time as ends in themselves. Hence results a systematic union of rational being by common objective laws, *i.e.*, a kingdom which may be called a kingdom of ends, since what these laws have in view is just the relation of these beings to one another as ends and means. It is certainly only an ideal.

A rational being belongs as a member to the kingdom of ends when, although giving universal laws in it, he is also himself subject to these laws. He belongs to it as sovereign when, while giving laws, he is not subject to the will of any other.

A rational being must always regard himself as giving laws either as member or as sovereign in a kingdom of ends which is rendered possible by the freedom of will. He cannot, however, maintain the latter position merely by the maxims of his will, but only in case he is a completely independent being without wants and with unrestricted power adequate to his will.

Morality consists then in the reference of all action to the legislation which alone can render a kingdom of ends possible. This legislation must be capable of existing in every rational being and of emanating from his will, so that the principle of this will is never to act on any maxim which could not without contradiction be also a universal law and, accordingly, always so to act that the will could at the same time regard itself as giving in its maxims universal laws. If now the maxims of rational beings are not by their own nature coincident with this objective principle, then the necessity of acting on it is called practical necessitation, *i.e.*, duty. Duty does not apply to the sovereign in the kingdom of ends, but it does to every member of it and to all in the same degree.

The practical necessity of acting on this principle, *i.e.*, duty, does not rest at all on feelings, impulses, or inclinations, but solely on the relation of rational beings to one another, a relation in which the will of a rational being must always be regarded as legislative, since otherwise it could not be conceived as an end in itself. Reason then refers every maxim of the will, regarding it as legislating universally, to every other will and also to every action towards oneself; and this not on account of any other practical motive or any future advantage, but from the idea of the dignity of a rational being, obeying no law but that which he himself also gives.

In the kingdom of ends everything has either value or dignity. Whatever has a value can be replaced by something else which is equivalent; whatever, on the other hand, is above all value, and therefore admits of no equivalent, has a dignity.

Whatever has reference to the general inclinations and wants of mankind has a market value; whatever, without presupposing a want, corresponds to a certain taste, that is to a satisfaction in the mere purposeless play of our faculties, has a fancy value; but that which constitutes the condition under which alone anything can be an end in itself, this has not merely a relative worth, *i.e.*, value, but an intrinsic worth, that is, dignity.

Now morality is the condition under which alone a rational being can be an end in himself, since by this alone is it possible that he should be a legislating member in the kingdom of ends. Thus morality, and humanity as capable of it, is that which alone has dignity. Skill and diligence in labour have a market value; wit, lively imagination, and humour, have fancy value; on the other hand, fidelity to promises, benevolence from principle (not from instinct), have an intrinsic worth. Neither nature nor art contains anything which in default of these it could put in their place, for their worth consists not in the effects which spring from them, not in the use and advantage which they secure, but in the disposition of mind, that is, the maxims of the will which are ready to manifest themselves in such actions, even though they should not have the desired effect. These actions also need no recommendation from any subjective taste or sentiment, that they may be looked on with immediate favour and satisfaction: they need no immediate propension or feeling for them; they exhibit the will that performs them as an object of an immediate respect, and nothing but reason is required to impose them on the will; not to flatter it into them, which, in the case of duties, would be a contradiction. This estimation therefore shows that the worth of such a disposition is dignity, and places it infinitely above all value, with which it cannot for a moment be brought into comparison or competition without as it were violating its sanctity.

What then is it which justifies virtue or the morally good disposition, in making such lofty claims? It is nothing less than the privilege it secures to the rational being of participating in the giving of universal laws, by which it qualifies him to be a member of a possible kingdom of ends, a privilege to which he was already destined by his own nature as being an end in himself and, on that account, legislating in the kingdom of ends; free as regards all laws of physical nature, and obeying those only which he himself gives, and by which his maxims can belong to a system of universal law, to which at the same time he submits himself. For nothing has any worth except what the law assigns it. Now the legislation itself which assigns the worth of everything must for that very reason possess dignity, that is an unconditional incomparable worth; and the word respect alone supplies a becoming expression for the esteem which a rational being must have for it. Autonomy then is the basis of the dignity of human and of every rational nature.

The three modes of presenting the principle of morality that have been adduced are at bottom only so many formulae of the very same law, and each of itself involves the other two. There is, however, a difference in them, but it is rather subjectively than objectively practical, intended namely to bring an idea of the reason nearer to intuition (by means of a certain analogy) and thereby nearer to feeling. All maxims, in fact, have:

1. A form, consisting in universality; and in this view the formula of the moral imperative is expressed thus, that the maxims must be so chosen as if they were to serve as universal laws of nature.

2. A matter, namely, an end, and here the formula says that the rational being, as it is an end by its own nature and therefore an end in itself, must in every maxim serve as the condition limiting all merely relative and arbitrary ends.

3. A complete characterization of all maxims by means of that formula, namely, that all maxims ought by their own legislation to harmonize with a possible kingdom of ends as with a kingdom of nature.[15] There is a progress here in the order of the categories of unity of the form of the will (its universality), plurality of the matter (the objects, *i.e.*, the ends), and totality of the system of these. In forming our moral judgement of actions, it is better to proceed always on the strict method and start from the general formula of the categorical imperative: Act according to a maxim which can at the same time make itself a universal law. If, however, we wish to gain an entrance for the moral law, it is very useful to bring one and the same action under the three specified conceptions, and thereby as far as possible to bring it nearer to intuition.

---

[15] Teleology considers nature as a kingdom of ends; ethics regards a possible kingdom of ends as a kingdom nature. In the first case, the kingdom of ends is a theoretical idea, adopted to explain what actually is. In the latter it is a practical idea, adopted to bring about that which is not yet, but which can be realized by our conduct, namely, if it conforms to this idea.

We can now end where we started at the beginning, namely, with the conception of a will unconditionally good. That will is absolutely good which cannot be evil- in other words, whose maxim, if made a universal law, could never contradict itself. This principle, then, is its supreme law: "Act always on such a maxim as thou canst at the same time will to be a universal law"; this is the sole condition under which a will can never contradict itself; and such an imperative is categorical. Since the validity of the will as a universal law for possible actions is analogous to the universal connexion of the existence of things by general laws, which is the formal notion of nature in general, the categorical imperative can also be expressed thus: Act on maxims which can at the same time have for their object themselves as universal laws of nature. Such then is the formula of an absolutely good will.

Rational nature is distinguished from the rest of nature by this, that it sets before itself an end. This end would be the matter of every good will. But since in the idea of a will that is absolutely good without being limited by any condition (of attaining this or that end) we must abstract wholly from every end to be effected (since this would make every will only relatively good), it follows that in this case the end must be conceived, not as an end to be effected, but as an independently existing end. Consequently it is conceived only negatively, *i.e.*, as that which we must never act against and which, therefore, must never be regarded merely as means, but must in every volition be esteemed as an end likewise. Now this end can be nothing but the subject of all possible ends, since this is also the subject of a possible absolutely good will; for such a will cannot without contradiction be postponed to any other object. The principle: "So act in regard to every rational being (thyself and others), that he may always have place in thy maxim as an end in himself," is accordingly essentially identical with this other: "Act upon a maxim which, at the same time, involves its own universal validity for every rational being." For that in using means for every end I should limit my maxim by the condition of its holding good as a law for every subject, this comes to the same thing as that the fundamental principle of all maxims of action must be that the subject of all ends, *i.e.*, the rational being himself, be never employed merely as means, but as the supreme condition restricting the use of all means, that is in every case as an end likewise.

It follows incontestably that, to whatever laws any rational being may be subject, he being an end in himself must be able to regard himself as also legislating universally in respect of these same laws, since it is just this fitness of his maxims for universal legislation that distinguishes him as an end in himself; also it follows that this implies his dignity (prerogative) above all mere physical beings, that he must always take his maxims from the point of view which regards himself and, likewise, every other rational being as law-giving beings (on which account they are called persons). In this way a world of rational beings (mundus intelligibilis) is possible as a kingdom of ends, and this by virtue of the legislation proper to all persons as members. Therefore every rational being must so act as if he were by his maxims in every case a legislating member in the universal kingdom of ends. The formal principle of these maxims is: "So act as if thy maxim were to serve likewise as the universal law (of all rational beings)." A kingdom of ends is thus only possible on the analogy of a kingdom of nature, the former however only by maxims, that is self-imposed rules, the latter only by the laws of efficient causes acting under necessitation from without. Nevertheless, although the system of nature is looked upon as a machine, yet so far as it has reference to rational beings as its ends, it is given on this account the name of a kingdom of nature. Now such a kingdom of ends would be actually realized by means of maxims conforming to the canon which the categorical imperative prescribes to all rational beings, if they were universally followed. But although a rational being, even if he punctually follows this maxim himself, cannot reckon upon all others being therefore true to the same, nor expect that the kingdom of nature and its orderly arrangements shall be in harmony with him as a fitting member, so as to form a kingdom of ends to which he himself contributes, that is to say, that it shall favour his expectation of happiness, still that law: "Act according to the maxims of a member of a merely possible kingdom of ends legislating in it universally," remains in its full force, inasmuch as it commands categorically. And it is just in this that the paradox lies; that the mere dignity of man as a rational creature, without any other end or advantage to be attained thereby, in other words, respect for a mere idea, should yet serve as an inflexible precept of the will, and that it is precisely in this independence of the maxim on all such springs of action that its sublimity consists; and it is this that makes every rational subject worthy to be a legislative member in the kingdom of ends: for otherwise he would have to be conceived only as subject to the physical law of his wants. And although we should suppose the kingdom of nature and the kingdom of ends to be united under one sovereign, so that the latter kingdom thereby ceased to be a mere idea and acquired true reality, then it would no doubt gain the accession of a strong spring, but by no means any increase of its intrinsic worth. For this sole absolute lawgiver must, notwithstanding this, be always conceived as estimating the worth of rational beings only by their disinterested behavior, as prescribed to themselves from that idea [the dignity of man] alone. The essence of things is not altered by their external relations, and that which, abstracting from these, alone constitutes the absolute worth of man, is also that by which he must be judged, whoever the judge may be, and even by the Supreme Being. Morality, then, is the relation of actions to the relation of actions will, that is, to the autonomy of potential universal legislation by its maxims. An action that is consistent with the autonomy of the will is permitted; one that does not agree therewith is forbidden. A will whose maxims necessarily coincide with the laws of autonomy is a holy will, good absolutely. The dependence of a will not absolutely good on the principle of autonomy (moral necessitation) is obligation. This, then, cannot be applied to a holy being. The objective necessity of actions from obligation is called duty.

From what has just been said, it is easy to see how it happens that, although the conception of duty implies subjection to the law, we yet ascribe a certain dignity and sublimity to the person who fulfils all his duties. There is not, indeed, any sublimity in him, so far as he is subject to the moral law; but inasmuch as in regard to that very law he is likewise a legislator, and on that account alone subject to it, he has sublimity. We have also shown above that neither fear nor inclination, but simply respect for the law, is the spring which can give actions a moral worth. Our own will, so far as we suppose it to act only under the condition that its maxims are potentially universal laws, this ideal will which is possible to us is the proper object of respect; and the dignity of humanity consists just in this capacity of being universally legislative, though with the condition that it is itself subject to this same legislation.

The Autonomy of the Will as the Supreme Principle of Morality

Autonomy of the will is that property of it by which it is a law to itself (independently of any property of the objects of volition). The principle of autonomy then is: "Always so to choose that the same volition shall comprehend the maxims of our choice as a universal law." We cannot prove that this practical rule is an imperative, *i.e.*, that the will of every rational being is necessarily bound to it as a condition, by a mere analysis of the conceptions which occur in it, since it is a synthetical proposition; we must advance beyond the cognition of the objects to a critical examination of the subject, that is, of the pure practical reason, for this synthetic proposition which commands apodeictically must be capable of being cognized wholly a priori. This matter, however, does not belong to the present section. But that the principle of autonomy in question is the sole principle of morals can be readily shown by mere analysis of the conceptions of morality. For by this analysis we find that its principle must be a categorical imperative and that what this commands is neither more nor less than this very autonomy.

Heteronomy of the Will as the Source of all spurious Principles of Morality

If the will seeks the law which is to determine it anywhere else than in the fitness of its maxims to be universal laws of its own dictation, consequently if it goes out of itself and seeks this law in the character of any of its objects, there always results heteronomy. The will in that case does not give itself the law, but it is given by the object through its relation to the will. This relation, whether it rests on inclination or on conceptions of reason, only admits of hypothetical imperatives: "I ought to do something because I wish for something else." On the contrary, the moral, and therefore categorical, imperative says: "I ought to do so and so, even though I should not wish for anything else." E.g., the former says: "I ought not to lie, if I would retain my reputation"; the latter says: "I ought not to lie, although it should not bring me the least discredit." The latter therefore must so far abstract from all objects that they shall have no influence on the will, in order that practical reason (will) may not be restricted to administering an interest not belonging to it, but may simply show its own commanding authority as the supreme legislation. Thus, e.g., I ought to endeavor to promote the happiness of others, not as if its realization involved any concern of mine (whether by immediate inclination or by any satisfaction indirectly gained through reason), but simply because a maxim which excludes it cannot be comprehended as a universal law in one and the same volition.

Classification of all Principles of Morality which can be founded on the Conception of Heteronomy

Here as elsewhere human reason in its pure use, so long as it was not critically examined, has first tried all possible wrong ways before it succeeded in finding the one true way.

All principles which can be taken from this point of view are either empirical or rational. The former, drawn from the principle of happiness, are built on physical or moral feelings; the latter, drawn from the principle of perfection, are built either on the rational conception of perfection as a possible effect, or on that of an independent perfection (the will of God) as the determining cause of our will.

Empirical principles are wholly incapable of serving as a foundation for moral laws. For the universality with which these should hold for all rational beings without distinction, the unconditional practical necessity which is thereby imposed on them, is lost when their foundation is taken from the particular constitution of human nature, or the accidental circumstances in which it is placed. The principle of private happiness, however, is the most objectionable, not merely because it is false, and experience contradicts the supposition that prosperity is always proportioned to good conduct, nor yet merely because it contributes nothing to the establishment of morality- since it is quite a different thing to make a prosperous man and a good man, or to make one prudent and sharp-sighted for his own interests and to make him virtuous- but because the springs it provides for morality are such as rather undermine it and destroy its sublimity, since they put the motives to virtue and to vice in the same class and only teach us to make a better calculation, the specific difference between virtue and vice being entirely extinguished. On the other hand, as to moral feeling, this supposed special sense,[16] the appeal to it is indeed superficial when those who cannot think believe that feeling will help them out, even in what concerns general laws: and besides, feelings, which naturally differ infinitely in degree, cannot furnish a uniform standard of good and evil, nor has anyone a right to form judgements for others by his own feelings: nevertheless this moral feeling is nearer to morality and its dignity in this respect, that it pays virtue the honour of ascribing to

---

[16] I class the principle of moral feeling under that of happiness, because every empirical interest promises to contribute to our well-being by the agreeableness that a thing affords, whether it be immediately and without a view to profit, or whether profit be regarded. We must likewise, with Hutcheson, class the principle of sympathy with the happiness of others under his assumed moral sense.

her immediately the satisfaction and esteem we have for her and does not, as it were, tell her to her face that we are not attached to her by her beauty but by profit.

Amongst the rational principles of morality, the ontological conception of perfection, notwithstanding its defects, is better than the theological conception which derives morality from a Divine absolutely perfect will. The former is, no doubt, empty and indefinite and consequently useless for finding in the boundless field of possible reality the greatest amount suitable for us; moreover, in attempting to distinguish specifically the reality of which we are now speaking from every other, it inevitably tends to turn in a circle and cannot avoid tacitly presupposing the morality which it is to explain; it is nevertheless preferable to the theological view, first, because we have no intuition of the divine perfection and can only deduce it from our own conceptions, the most important of which is that of morality, and our explanation would thus be involved in a gross circle; and, in the next place, if we avoid this, the only notion of the Divine will remaining to us is a conception made up of the attributes of desire of glory and dominion, combined with the awful conceptions of might and vengeance, and any system of morals erected on this foundation would be directly opposed to morality.

However, if I had to choose between the notion of the moral sense and that of perfection in general (two systems which at least do not weaken morality, although they are totally incapable of serving as its foundation), then I should decide for the latter, because it at least withdraws the decision of the question from the sensibility and brings it to the court of pure reason; and although even here it decides nothing, it at all events preserves the indefinite idea (of a will good in itself free from corruption, until it shall be more precisely defined.

For the rest I think I may be excused here from a detailed refutation of all these doctrines; that would only be superfluous labour, since it is so easy, and is probably so well seen even by those whose office requires them to decide for one of these theories (because their hearers would not tolerate suspension of judgement). But what interests us more here is to know that the prime foundation of morality laid down by all these principles is nothing but heteronomy of the will, and for this reason they must necessarily miss their aim.

In every case where an object of the will has to be supposed, in order that the rule may be prescribed which is to determine the will, there the rule is simply heteronomy; the imperative is conditional, namely, if or because one wishes for this object, one should act so and so: hence it can never command morally, that is, categorically. Whether the object determines the will by means of inclination, as in the principle of private happiness, or by means of reason directed to objects of our possible volition generally, as in the principle of perfection, in either case the will never determines itself immediately by the conception of the action, but only by the influence which the foreseen effect of the action has on the will; I ought to do something, on this account, because I wish for something else; and here there must be yet another law assumed in me as its subject, by which I necessarily will this other thing, and this law again requires an imperative to restrict this maxim. For the influence which the conception of an object within the reach of our faculties can exercise on the will of the subject, in consequence of its natural properties, depends on the nature of the subject, either the sensibility (inclination and taste), or the understanding and reason, the employment of which is by the peculiar constitution of their nature attended with satisfaction. It follows that the law would be, properly speaking, given by nature, and, as such, it must be known and proved by experience and would consequently be contingent and therefore incapable of being an apodeictic practical rule, such as the moral rule must be. Not only so, but it is inevitably only heteronomy; the will does not give itself the law, but is given by a foreign impulse by means of a particular natural constitution of the subject adapted to receive it. An absolutely good will, then, the principle of which must be a categorical imperative, will be indeterminate as regards all objects and will contain merely the form of volition generally, and that as autonomy, that is to say, the capability of the maxims of every good will to make themselves a universal law, is itself the only law which the will of every rational being imposes on itself, without needing to assume any spring or interest as a foundation.

How such a synthetical practical a priori proposition is possible, and why it is necessary, is a problem whose solution does not lie within the bounds of the metaphysic of morals; and we have not here affirmed its truth, much less professed to have a proof of it in our power. We simply showed by the development of the universally received notion of morality that an autonomy of the will is inevitably connected with it, or rather is its foundation. Whoever then holds morality to be anything real, and not a chimerical idea without any truth, must likewise admit the principle of it that is here assigned. This section then, like the first, was merely analytical. Now to prove that morality is no creation of the brain, which it cannot be if the categorical imperative and with it the autonomy of the will is true, and as an a priori principle absolutely necessary, this supposes the possibility of a synthetic use of pure practical reason, which however we cannot venture on without first giving a critical examination of this faculty of reason. In the concluding section we shall give the principal outlines of this critical examination as far as is sufficient for our purpose.

Third Section

Transition From The Metaphysic Of Morals To The Critique Of Pure Practical Reason

The Concept of Freedom is the Key that explains the Autonomy of the Will

The will is a kind of causality belonging to living beings in so far as they are rational, and freedom would be this property of such causality that it can be efficient, independently of foreign causes determining it; just as physical necessity is the property that the causality of all irrational beings has of being determined to activity by the influence of foreign causes.

The preceding definition of freedom is negative and therefore unfruitful for the discovery of its essence, but it leads to a positive conception which is so much the more full and fruitful.

Since the conception of causality involves that of laws, according to which, by something that we call cause, something else, namely the effect, must be produced; hence, although freedom is not a property of the will depending on physical laws, yet it is not for that reason lawless; on the contrary it must be a causality acting according to immutable laws, but of a peculiar kind; otherwise a free will would be an absurdity. Physical necessity is a heteronomy of the efficient causes, for every effect is possible only according to this law, that something else determines the efficient cause to exert its causality. What else then can freedom of the will be but autonomy, that is, the property of the will to be a law to itself? But the proposition: "The will is in every action a law to itself," only expresses the principle: "To act on no other maxim than that which can also have as an object itself as a universal law." Now this is precisely the formula of the categorical imperative and is the principle of morality, so that a free will and a will subject to moral laws are one and the same.

On the hypothesis, then, of freedom of the will, morality together with its principle follows from it by mere analysis of the conception. However, the latter is a synthetic proposition; viz., an absolutely good will is that whose maxim can always include itself regarded as a universal law; for this property of its maxim can never be discovered by analysing the conception of an absolutely good will. Now such synthetic propositions are only possible in this way: that the two cognitions are connected together by their union with a third in which they are both to be found. The positive concept of freedom furnishes this third cognition, which cannot, as with physical causes, be the nature of the sensible world (in the concept of which we find conjoined the concept of something in relation as cause to something else as effect). We cannot now at once show what this third is to which freedom points us and of which we have an idea a priori, nor can we make intelligible how the concept of freedom is shown to be legitimate from principles of pure practical reason and with it the possibility of a categorical imperative; but some further preparation is required.

Freedom must be presupposed as a Property of the Will of all Rational Beings

It is not enough to predicate freedom of our own will, from Whatever reason, if we have not sufficient grounds for predicating the same of all rational beings. For as morality serves as a law for us only because we are rational beings, it must also hold for all rational beings; and as it must be deduced simply from the property of freedom, it must be shown that freedom also is a property of all rational beings. It is not enough, then, to prove it from certain supposed experiences of human nature (which indeed is quite impossible, and it can only be shown a priori), but we must show that it belongs to the activity of all rational beings endowed with a will. Now I say every being that cannot act except under the idea of freedom is just for that reason in a practical point of view really free, that is to say, all laws which are inseparably connected with freedom have the same force for him as if his will had been shown to be free in itself by a proof theoretically conclusive.[17] Now I affirm that we must attribute to every rational being which has a will that it has also the idea of freedom and acts entirely under this idea. For in such a being we conceive a reason that is practical, that is, has causality in reference to its objects. Now we cannot possibly conceive a reason consciously receiving a bias from any other quarter with respect to its judgements, for then the subject would ascribe the determination of its judgement not to its own reason, but to an impulse. It must regard itself as the author of its principles independent of foreign influences. Consequently as practical reason or as the will of a rational being it must regard itself as free, that is to say, the will of such a being cannot be a will of its own except under the idea of freedom. This idea must therefore in a practical point of view be ascribed to every rational being.

Of the Interest attaching to the Ideas of Morality

We have finally reduced the definite conception of morality to the idea of freedom. This latter, however, we could not prove to be actually a property of ourselves or of human nature; only we saw that it must be presupposed if we would conceive a being as rational and conscious of its causality in respect of its actions, *i.e.*, as endowed with a will; and so we find that on just the same grounds we must ascribe

---

[17] I adopt this method of assuming freedom merely as an idea which rational beings suppose in their actions, in order to avoid the necessity of proving it in its theoretical aspect also. The former is sufficient for my purpose; for even though the speculative proof should not be made out, yet a being that cannot act except with the idea of freedom is bound by the same laws that would oblige a being who was actually free. Thus we can escape here from the onus which presses on the theory.

to every being endowed with reason and will this attribute of determining itself to action under the idea of its freedom.

Now it resulted also from the presupposition of these ideas that we became aware of a law that the subjective principles of action, *i.e.*, maxims, must always be so assumed that they can also hold as objective, that is, universal principles, and so serve as universal laws of our own dictation. But why then should I subject myself to this principle and that simply as a rational being, thus also subjecting to it all other being endowed with reason? I will allow that no interest urges me to this, for that would not give a categorical imperative, but I must take an interest in it and discern how this comes to pass; for this properly an "I ought" is properly an "I would," valid for every rational being, provided only that reason determined his actions without any hindrance. But for beings that are in addition affected as we are by springs of a different kind, namely, sensibility, and in whose case that is not always done which reason alone would do, for these that necessity is expressed only as an "ought," and the subjective necessity is different from the objective.

It seems then as if the moral law, that is, the principle of autonomy of the will, were properly speaking only presupposed in the idea of freedom, and as if we could not prove its reality and objective necessity independently. In that case we should still have gained something considerable by at least determining the true principle more exactly than had previously been done; but as regards its validity and the practical necessity of subjecting oneself to it, we should not have advanced a step. For if we were asked why the universal validity of our maxim as a law must be the condition restricting our actions, and on what we ground the worth which we assign to this manner of acting- a worth so great that there cannot be any higher interest; and if we were asked further how it happens that it is by this alone a man believes he feels his own personal worth, in comparison with which that of an agreeable or disagreeable condition is to be regarded as nothing, to these questions we could give no satisfactory answer.

We find indeed sometimes that we can take an interest in a personal quality which does not involve any interest of external condition, provided this quality makes us capable of participating in the condition in case reason were to effect the allotment; that is to say, the mere being worthy of happiness can interest of itself even without the motive of participating in this happiness. This judgement, however, is in fact only the effect of the importance of the moral law which we before presupposed (when by the idea of freedom we detach ourselves from every empirical interest); but that we ought to detach ourselves from these interests, *i.e.*, to consider ourselves as free in action and yet as subject to certain laws, so as to find a worth simply in our own person which can compensate us for the loss of everything that gives worth to our condition; this we are not yet able to discern in this way, nor do we see how it is possible so to act- in other words, whence the moral law derives its obligation.

It must be freely admitted that there is a sort of circle here from which it seems impossible to escape. In the order of efficient causes we assume ourselves free, in order that in the order of ends we may conceive ourselves as subject to moral laws:

and we afterwards conceive ourselves as subject to these laws, because we have attributed to ourselves freedom of will: for freedom and self-legislation of will are both autonomy and, therefore, are reciprocal conceptions, and for this very reason one must not be used to explain the other or give the reason of it, but at most only logical purposes to reduce apparently different notions of the same object to one single concept (as we reduce different fractions of the same value to the lowest terms).

One resource remains to us, namely, to inquire whether we do not occupy different points of view when by means of freedom we think ourselves as causes efficient a priori, and when we form our conception of ourselves from our actions as effects which we see before our eyes.

It is a remark which needs no subtle reflection to make, but which we may assume that even the commonest understanding can make, although it be after its fashion by an obscure discernment of judgement which it calls feeling, that all the "ideas" that come to us involuntarily (as those of the senses) do not enable us to know objects otherwise than as they affect us; so that what they may be in themselves remains unknown to us, and consequently that as regards "ideas" of this kind even with the closest attention and clearness that the understanding can apply to them, we can by them only attain to the knowledge of appearances, never to that of things in themselves. As soon as this distinction has once been made (perhaps merely in consequence of the difference observed between the ideas given us from without, and in which we are passive, and those that we produce simply from ourselves, and in which we show our own activity), then it follows of itself that we must admit and assume behind the appearance something else that is not an appearance, namely, the things in themselves; although we must admit that as they can never be known to us except as they affect us, we can come no nearer to them, nor can we ever know what they are in themselves. This must furnish a distinction, however crude, between a world of sense and the world of understanding, of which the former may be different according to the difference of the sensuous impressions in various observers, while the second which is its basis always remains the same, Even as to himself, a man cannot pretend to know what he is in himself from the knowledge he has by internal sensation. For as he does not as it were create himself, and does not come by the conception of himself a priori but empirically, it naturally follows that he can obtain his knowledge even of himself only by the inner sense and, consequently, only through the appearances of his nature and the way in which his consciousness is affected. At the same time beyond these characteristics of his own subject, made up of mere appearances, he must necessarily suppose something else as their basis, namely, his ego, whatever its characteristics in itself may be. Thus in respect to mere perception and receptivity of sensations he must reckon himself as belonging to the world of sense; but in respect of whatever there may be of pure activity in him (that which reaches consciousness immediately and not through affecting the senses), he must reckon himself as belonging to the intellectual world, of which, however, he has no further knowledge. To such a conclusion the reflecting man must come with respect to all the things which can be presented to him: it is probably to be met with even in persons of the commonest understanding, who, as is well known, are very much inclined to suppose behind the objects of the senses something else invisible and acting of itself. They spoil it, however, by presently sensualizing this invisible again; that is to say, wanting to make it an object of intuition, so that they do not become a whit the wiser.

Now man really finds in himself a faculty by which he distinguishes himself from everything else, even from himself as affected by objects, and that is reason. This being pure spontaneity is even elevated above the understanding. For although the latter is a spontaneity and does not, like sense, merely contain intuitions that arise when we are affected by things (and are therefore passive), yet it cannot produce from its activity any other conceptions than those which merely serve to bring the intuitions of sense under rules and, thereby, to unite them in one consciousness, and without this use of the sensibility it could not think at all; whereas, on the contrary, reason shows so pure a spontaneity in the case of what I call ideas [ideal conceptions] that it thereby far transcends everything that the sensibility can give it, and exhibits its most important function in distinguishing the world of sense from that of understanding, and thereby prescribing the limits of the understanding itself.

For this reason a rational being must regard himself qua intelligence (not from the side of his lower faculties) as belonging not to the world of sense, but to that of understanding; hence he has two points of view from which he can regard himself, and recognize laws of the exercise of his faculties, and consequently of all his actions: first, so far as he belongs to the world of sense, he finds himself subject to laws of nature (heteronomy); secondly, as belonging to the intelligible world, under laws which being independent of nature have their foundation not in experience but in reason alone.

As a rational being, and consequently belonging to the intelligible world, man can never conceive the causality of his own will otherwise than on condition of the idea of freedom, for independence of the determinate causes of the sensible world (an independence which reason must always ascribe to itself) is freedom. Now the idea of freedom is inseparably connected with the conception of autonomy, and this again with the universal principle of morality which is ideally the foundation of all actions of rational beings, just as the law of nature is of all phenomena.

Now the suspicion is removed which we raised above, that there was a latent circle involved in our reasoning from freedom to autonomy, and from this to the moral law, viz.: that we laid down the idea of freedom because of the moral law only that we might afterwards in turn infer the latter from freedom, and that consequently we could assign no reason at all for this law, but could only [present] it as a *petitio principii* which well disposed minds would gladly concede to us, but which we could never put forward as a provable proposition. For now we see that, when we conceive ourselves as free, we transfer ourselves into the world of understanding as members of it and recognise the autonomy of the will with its consequence, morality; whereas, if we conceive ourselves as under obligation, we consider ourselves as belonging to the world of sense and at the same time to the world of understanding.

How is a Categorical Imperative Possible?

Every rational being reckons himself qua intelligence as belonging to the world of understanding, and it is simply as an efficient cause belonging to that world that he calls his causality a will. On the other side he is also conscious of himself as a part of the world of sense in which his actions, which are mere appearances [phenomena] of that causality, are displayed; we cannot, however, discern how they are possible from this causality which we do not know; but instead of that, these actions as belonging to the sensible world must be viewed as determined by other phenomena, namely, desires and inclinations. If therefore I were only a member of the world of understanding, then all my actions would perfectly conform to the principle of autonomy of the pure will; if I were only a part of the world of sense, they would necessarily be assumed to conform wholly to the natural law of desires and inclinations, in other words, to the heteronomy of nature. (The former would rest on morality as the supreme principle, the latter on happiness.) Since, however, the world of understanding contains the foundation of the world of sense, and consequently of its laws also, and accordingly gives the law to my will (which belongs wholly to the world of understanding) directly, and must be conceived as doing so, it follows that, although on the one side I must regard myself as a being belonging to the world of sense, yet on the other side I must recognize myself as subject as an intelligence to the law of the world of understanding, *i.e.*, to reason, which contains this law in the idea of freedom, and therefore as subject to the autonomy of the will: consequently I must regard the laws of the world of understanding as imperatives for me and the actions which conform to them as duties.

And thus what makes categorical imperatives possible is this, that the idea of freedom makes me a member of an intelligible world, in consequence of which, if I were nothing else, all my actions would always conform to the autonomy of the will; but as I at the same time intuite myself as a member of the world of sense, they ought so to conform, and this categorical "ought" implies a synthetic a priori proposition, inasmuch as besides my will as affected by sensible desires there is added further the idea of the same will but as belonging to the world of the understanding, pure and practical of itself, which contains the supreme condition according to reason of the former will; precisely as to the intuitions of sense there are added concepts of the understanding which of themselves signify nothing but regular form in general and in this way synthetic a priori propositions become possible, on which all knowledge of physical nature rests.

The practical use of common human reason confirms this reasoning. There is no one, not even the most consummate villain, provided only that he is otherwise accustomed to the use of reason, who, when we set before him examples of honesty of purpose, of steadfastness in following good maxims, of sympathy and general benevolence (even combined with great sacrifices of advantages and comfort), does not wish that he might also possess these qualities. Only on account of his inclinations and impulses he cannot attain this in himself, but at the same time he wishes to be free from such inclinations which are burdensome to himself. He proves by this that he transfers himself in thought with a will free from the impulses of the sensibility into an order of things wholly different from that of his desires in the field of the sensibility; since he cannot expect to obtain by that wish any gratification of his desires, nor any position which would satisfy any of his actual or supposable inclinations (for this would destroy the pre-eminence of the very idea which wrests that wish from him): he can only expect a greater intrinsic worth of his own person. This better person, however, he imagines himself to be when be transfers himself to the point of view of a member of the world of the understanding, to which he is involuntarily forced by the idea of freedom, *i.e.*, of independence on determining causes of the world of sense; and from this point of view he is conscious of a good will, which by his own confession constitutes the law for the bad will that he possesses as a member of the world of sense- a law whose authority he recognizes while transgressing it. What he morally "ought" is then what he necessarily "would," as a member of the world of the understanding, and is conceived by him as an "ought" only inasmuch as he likewise considers himself as a member of the world of sense.

Of the Extreme Limits of all Practical Philosophy

All men attribute to themselves freedom of will. Hence come all judgements upon actions as being such as ought to have been done, although they have not been done. However, this freedom is not a conception of experience, nor can it be so, since it still remains, even though experience shows the contrary of what on supposition of freedom are conceived as its necessary consequences. On the other side it is equally necessary that everything that takes place should be fixedly determined according to laws of nature. This necessity of nature is likewise not an empirical conception, just for this reason, that it involves the motion of necessity and consequently of a priori cognition. But this conception of a system of nature is confirmed by experience; and it must even be inevitably presupposed if experience itself is to be possible, that is, a connected knowledge of the objects of sense resting on general laws. Therefore freedom is only an idea of reason, and its objective reality in itself is doubtful; while nature is a concept of the understanding which proves, and must necessarily prove, its reality in examples of experience.

There arises from this a dialectic of reason, since the freedom attributed to the will appears to contradict the necessity of nature, and placed between these two ways reason for speculative purposes finds the road of physical necessity much more beaten and more appropriate than that of freedom; yet for practical purposes the narrow footpath of freedom is the only one on which it is possible to make use of reason in our conduct; hence it is just as impossible for the subtlest philosophy as for the commonest reason of men to argue away freedom. Philosophy must then assume that no real contradiction will be found between freedom and physical necessity of the same human actions, for it cannot give up the conception of nature any more than that of freedom.

Nevertheless, even though we should never be able to comprehend how freedom is possible, we must at least remove this apparent contradiction in a convincing manner. For if the thought of freedom contradicts either itself or nature, which is equally necessary, it must in competition with physical necessity be entirely given up.

It would, however, be impossible to escape this contradiction if the thinking subject, which seems to itself free, conceived itself in the same sense or in the very same relation when it calls itself free as when in respect of the same action it assumes itself to be subject to the law of nature. Hence it is an indispensable problem of speculative philosophy to show that its illusion respecting the contradiction rests on this, that we think of man in a different sense and relation when we call him free and when we regard him as subject to the laws of nature as being part and parcel of nature. It must therefore show that not only can both these very well co-exist, but that both must be thought as necessarily united in the same subject, since otherwise no reason could be given why we should burden reason with an idea which, though it may possibly without contradiction be reconciled with another that is sufficiently established, yet entangles us in a perplexity which sorely embarrasses reason in its theoretic employment. This duty, however, belongs only to speculative philosophy. The philosopher then has no option whether he will remove the apparent contradiction or leave it untouched; for in the latter case the theory respecting this would be *bonum vacans*, into the possession of which the fatalist would have a right to enter and chase all morality out of its supposed domain as occupying it without title.

We cannot however as yet say that we are touching the bounds of practical philosophy. For the settlement of that controversy does not belong to it; it only demands from speculative reason that it should put an end to the discord in which it entangles itself in theoretical questions, so that practical reason may have rest and security from external attacks which might make the ground debatable on which it desires to build.

The claims to freedom of will made even by common reason are founded on the consciousness and the admitted supposition that reason is independent of merely subjectively determined causes which together constitute what belongs to sensation only and which consequently come under the general designation of sensibility. Man considering himself in this way as an intelligence places himself thereby in a different order of things and in a relation to determining grounds of a wholly different kind when on the one hand he thinks of himself as an intelligence endowed with a will, and consequently with causality, and when on the other he perceives himself as a phenomenon in the world of sense (as he really is also), and affirms that his causality is subject to external determination according to laws of nature. Now he soon becomes aware that both can hold good, nay, must hold good at the same time. For there is not the smallest contradiction in saying that a thing in appearance (belonging to the world of sense) is subject to certain laws, of which the very same as a thing or being in itself is independent, and that he must conceive and think of himself in this twofold way, rests as to the first on the consciousness of himself as an object affected through the senses, and as to the second on the consciousness of himself as an intelligence, *i.e.*, as independent on sensible impressions in the employment of his reason (in other words as belonging to the world of understanding).

Hence it comes to pass that man claims the possession of a will which takes no account of anything that comes under the head of desires and inclinations and, on the contrary, conceives actions as possible to him, nay, even as necessary which can only be done by disregarding all desires and sensible inclinations. The causality of such actions lies in him as an intelligence and in the laws of effects and actions [which depend] on the principles of an intelligible world, of which indeed he knows nothing more than that in it pure reason alone independent of sensibility gives the law; moreover since it is only in that world, as an intelligence, that he is his proper self (being as man only the appearance of himself), those laws apply to him directly and categorically, so that the incitements of inclinations and appetites (in other words the whole nature of the world of sense) cannot impair the laws of his volition as an intelligence. Nay, he does not even hold himself responsible for the former or ascribe them to his proper self, *i.e.*, his will: he only ascribes to his will any indulgence which he might yield them if he allowed them to influence his maxims to the prejudice of the rational laws of the will.

When practical reason thinks itself into a world of understanding, it does not thereby transcend its own limits, as it would if it tried to enter it by intuition or sensation. The former is only a negative thought in respect of the world of sense, which does not give any laws to reason in determining the will and is positive only in this single point that this freedom as a negative characteristic is at the same time conjoined with a (positive) faculty and even with a causality of reason, which we designate a will, namely a faculty of so acting that the principle of the actions shall conform to the essential character of a rational motive, *i.e.*, the condition that the maxim have universal validity as a law. But were it to borrow an object of will, that is, a motive, from the world of understanding, then it would overstep its bounds and pretend to be acquainted with something of which it knows nothing. The conception of a world of the understanding is then only a point of view which reason finds itself compelled to take outside the appearances in order to conceive itself as practical, which would not be possible if the influences of the sensibility had a determining power on man, but which is necessary unless he is to be denied the consciousness of himself as an intelligence and, consequently, as a rational cause, energizing by reason, that is, operating freely. This thought certainly involves the idea of an order and a system of laws different from that of the mechanism of nature which belongs to the sensible world; and it makes the conception of an intelligible world necessary (that is to say, the whole system of rational beings as things in themselves). But it does not in the least authorize us to think of it further than as to its formal condition only, that is, the universality of the maxims of the will as laws, and consequently the autonomy of the latter, which alone is consistent with its freedom; whereas, on the contrary, all laws that refer to a definite object give heteronomy, which only belongs to laws of nature and can only apply to the sensible world.

But reason would overstep all its bounds if it undertook to explain how pure reason can be practical, which would be exactly the same problem as to explain how freedom is possible.

For we can explain nothing but that which we can reduce to laws, the object of which can be given in some possible experience. But freedom is a mere idea, the objective reality of which can in no wise be shown according to laws of nature, and consequently not in any possible experience; and for this reason it can never be comprehended or understood, because we cannot support it by any sort of example or analogy. It holds good only as a necessary hypothesis of reason in a being that believes itself conscious of a will, that is, of a faculty distinct from mere desire (namely, a faculty of determining itself to action as an intelligence, in other words, by laws of reason independently on natural instincts). Now where determination according to laws of nature ceases, there all explanation ceases also, and nothing remains but defense, *i.e.*, the removal of the objections of those who pretend to have seen deeper into the nature of things, and thereupon boldly declare freedom impossible. We can only point out to them that the supposed contradiction that they have discovered in it arises only from this, that in order to be able to apply the law of nature to human actions, they must necessarily consider man as an appearance: then when we demand of them that they should also think of him qua intelligence as a thing in itself, they still persist in considering him in this respect also as an appearance. In this view it would no doubt be a contradiction to suppose the causality of the same subject (that is, his will) to be withdrawn from all the natural laws of the sensible world. But this contradiction disappears, if they would only bethink themselves and admit, as is reasonable, that behind the appearances there must also lie at their root (although hidden) the things in themselves, and that we cannot expect the laws of these to be the same as those that govern their appearances.

The subjective impossibility of explaining the freedom of the will is identical with the impossibility of discovering and explaining an interest[18] which man can take in the moral law. Nevertheless he does actually take an interest in it, the basis of which in us we call the moral feeling, which some have falsely assigned as the standard of our moral judgement, whereas it must rather be viewed as the subjective effect that

---

[18] Interest is that by which reason becomes practical, *i.e.*, a cause determining the will. Hence we say of rational beings only that they take an interest in a thing; irrational beings only feel sensual appetites. Reason takes a direct interest in action then only when the universal validity of its maxims is alone sufficient to determine the will. Such an interest alone is pure. But if it can determine the will only by means of another object of desire or on the suggestion of a particular feeling of the subject, then reason takes only an indirect interest in the action, and, as reason by itself without experience cannot discover either objects of the will or a special feeling actuating it, this latter interest would only be empirical and not a pure rational interest. The logical interest of reason (namely, to extend its insight) is never direct, but presupposes purposes for which reason is employed.

the law exercises on the will, the objective principle of which is furnished by reason alone.

In order indeed that a rational being who is also affected through the senses should will what reason alone directs such beings that they ought to will, it is no doubt requisite that reason should have a power to infuse a feeling of pleasure or satisfaction in the fulfillment of duty, that is to say, that it should have a causality by which it determines the sensibility according to its own principles. But it is quite impossible to discern, *i.e.*, to make it intelligible a priori, how a mere thought, which itself contains nothing sensible, can itself produce a sensation of pleasure or pain; for this is a particular kind of causality of which as of every other causality we can determine nothing whatever a priori; we must only consult experience about it. But as this cannot supply us with any relation of cause and effect except between two objects of experience, whereas in this case, although indeed the effect produced lies within experience, yet the cause is supposed to be pure reason acting through mere ideas which offer no object to experience, it follows that for us men it is quite impossible to explain how and why the universality of the maxim as a law, that is, morality, interests. This only is certain, that it is not because it interests us that it has validity for us (for that would be heteronomy and dependence of practical reason on sensibility, namely, on a feeling as its principle, in which case it could never give moral laws), but that it interests us because it is valid for us as men, inasmuch as it had its source in our will as intelligences, in other words, in our proper self, and what belongs to mere appearance is necessarily subordinated by reason to the nature of the thing in itself.

The question then, "How a categorical imperative is possible," can be answered to this extent, that we can assign the only hypothesis on which it is possible, namely, the idea of freedom; and we can also discern the necessity of this hypothesis, and this is sufficient for the practical exercise of reason, that is, for the conviction of the validity of this imperative, and hence of the moral law; but how this hypothesis itself is possible can never be discerned by any human reason. On the hypothesis, however, that the will of an intelligence is free, its autonomy, as the essential formal condition of its determination, is a necessary consequence. Moreover, this freedom of will is not merely quite possible as a hypothesis (not involving any contradiction to the principle of physical necessity in the connexion of the phenomena of the sensible world) as speculative philosophy can show: but further, a rational being who is conscious of causality through reason, that is to say, of a will (distinct from desires), must of necessity make it practically, that is, in idea, the condition of all his voluntary actions. But to explain how pure reason can be of itself practical without the aid of any spring of action that could be derived from any other source, *i.e.*, how the mere principle of the universal validity of all its maxims as laws (which would certainly be the form of a pure practical reason) can of itself supply a spring, without any matter (object) of the will in which one could antecedently take any interest; and how it can produce an interest which would be called purely moral; or in other words, how pure reason can be practical- to explain this is beyond the power of human reason, and all the labour and pains of seeking an explanation of it are lost.

It is just the same as if I sought to find out how freedom itself is possible as the causality of a will. For then I quit the ground of philosophical explanation, and I have no other to go upon. I might indeed revel in the world of intelligences which still remains to me, but although I have an idea of it which is well founded, yet I have not the least knowledge of it, nor an I ever attain to such knowledge with all the efforts of my natural faculty of reason. It signifies only a something that remains over when I have eliminated everything belonging to the world of sense from the actuating principles of my will, serving merely to keep in bounds the principle of motives taken from the field of sensibility; fixing its limits and showing that it does not contain all in all within itself, but that there is more beyond it; but this something more I know no further. Of pure reason which frames this ideal, there remains after the abstraction of all matter, *i.e.*, knowledge of objects, nothing but the form, namely, the practical law of the universality of the maxims, and in conformity with this conception of reason in reference to a pure world of understanding as a possible efficient cause, that is a cause determining the will. There must here be a total absence of springs; unless this idea of an intelligible world is itself the spring, or that in which reason primarily takes an interest; but to make this intelligible is precisely the problem that we cannot solve.

Here now is the extreme limit of all moral inquiry, and it is of great importance to determine it even on this account, in order that reason may not on the one band, to the prejudice of morals, seek about in the world of sense for the supreme motive and an interest comprehensible but empirical; and on the other hand, that it may not impotently flap its wings without being able to move in the (for it) empty space of transcendent concepts which we call the intelligible world, and so lose itself amidst chimeras. For the rest, the idea of a pure world of understanding as a system of all intelligences, and to which we ourselves as rational beings belong (although we are likewise on the other side members of the sensible world), this remains always a useful and legitimate idea for the purposes of rational belief, although all knowledge stops at its threshold, useful, namely, to produce in us a lively interest in the moral law by means of the noble ideal of a universal kingdom of ends in themselves (rational beings), to which we can belong as members then only when we carefully conduct ourselves according to the maxims of freedom as if they were laws of nature.

Concluding Remark

The speculative employment of reason with respect to nature leads to the absolute necessity of some supreme cause of the world: the practical employment of reason with a view to freedom leads also to absolute necessity, but only of the laws of the actions of a rational being as such. Now it is an essential principle of reason, however employed, to push its knowledge to a consciousness of its necessity (without which it would not be rational knowledge). It is, however, an equally essential restriction of the same reason that it can neither discern the necessity of what is or what happens, nor of what ought to happen, unless a condition is supposed on which it is or happens or ought to happen. In this way, however, by the constant inquiry for the condition, the satisfaction of reason is only further and further postponed. Hence it unceasingly seeks the unconditionally necessary and finds itself forced to assume it, although without any means of making it comprehensible to itself, happy enough if only it can discover a conception which agrees with this assumption. It is therefore no fault in our deduction of the supreme principle of morality, but an objection that should be made to human reason in general, that it cannot enable us to conceive the absolute necessity of an unconditional practical law (such as the categorical imperative must be). It cannot be blamed for refusing to explain this necessity by a condition, that is to say, by means of some interest assumed as a basis, since the law would then cease to be a supreme law of reason. And thus while we do not comprehend the practical unconditional necessity of the moral imperative, we yet comprehend its incomprehensibility, and this is all that can be fairly demanded of a philosophy which strives to carry its principles up to the very limit of human reason.

The End

The

Metaphysical Elements

Of

Ethics

by

Immanuel Kant

translated by
Thomas Kingsmill Abbott

PREFACE

If there exists on any subject a philosophy (that is, a system of rational knowledge based on concepts), then there must also be for this philosophy a system of pure rational concepts, independent of any condition of intuition, in other words, a metaphysic. It may be asked whether metaphysical elements are required also for every practical philosophy, which is the doctrine of duties, and therefore also for Ethics, in order to be able to present it as a true science (systematically), not merely as an aggregate of separate doctrines (fragmentarily). As regards pure jurisprudence, no one will question this requirement; for it concerns only what is formal in the elective will, which has to be limited in its external relations according to laws of freedom; without regarding any end which is the matter of this will. Here, therefore, deontology is a mere scientific doctrine (doctrina scientiae).[1]

Now in this philosophy (of ethics) it seems contrary to the idea of it that we should go back to metaphysical elements in order to make the notion of duty purified from everything empirical (from every feeling) a motive of action. For what sort of notion can we form of the mighty power and herculean strength which would be sufficient to overcome the vice-breeding inclinations, if Virtue is to borrow her "arms from the armoury of metaphysics," which is a matter of speculation that only few men can handle? Hence all ethical teaching in lecture rooms, pulpits, and popular books, when it is decked out with fragments of metaphysics, becomes ridiculous. But it is not, therefore, useless, much less ridiculous, to trace in metaphysics the first principles of ethics; for it is only as a philosopher that anyone can reach the first principles of this conception of duty, otherwise we could not look for either certainty or purity in the ethical teaching. To rely for this reason on a certain feeling which, on account of the effect expected from it, is called moral, may, perhaps, even satisfy the popular teacher, provided he desires as the criterion of a moral duty to consider the problem: "If everyone in every case made your maxim the universal law, how could

---

[1] One who is acquainted with practical philosophy is not, therefore, a practical philosopher. The latter is he who makes the rational end the principle of his actions, while at the same time he joins with this the necessary knowledge which, as it aims at action, must not be spun out into the most subtle threads of metaphysic, unless a legal duty is in question; in which case meum and tuum must be accurately determined in the balance of justice, on the principle of equality of action and action, which requires something like mathematical proportion, but not in the case of a mere ethical duty. For in this case the question is not only to know what it is a duty to do (a thing which on account of the ends that all men naturally have can be easily decided), but the chief point is the inner principle of the will namely that the consciousness of this duty be also the spring of action, in order that we may be able to say of the man who joins to his knowledge this principle of wisdom that he is a practical philosopher.

this law be consistent with itself?" But if it were merely feeling that made it our duty to take this principle as a criterion, then this would not be dictated by reason, but only adopted instinctively and therefore blindly.

But in fact, whatever men imagine, no moral principle is based on any feeling, but such a principle is really nothing else than an obscurely conceived metaphysic which inheres in every man's reasoning faculty; as the teacher will easily find who tries to catechize his pupils in the Socratic method about the imperative of duty and its application to the moral judgement of his actions. The mode of stating it need not be always metaphysical, and the language need not necessarily be scholastic, unless the pupil is to be trained to be a philosopher. But the thought must go back to the elements of metaphysics, without which we cannot expect any certainty or purity, or even motive power in ethics.

If we deviate from this principle and begin from pathological, or purely sensitive, or even moral feeling (from what is subjectively practical instead of what is objective), that is, from the matter of the will, the end, not from its form that is the law, in order from thence to determine duties; then, certainly, there are no metaphysical elements of ethics, for feeling by whatever it may be excited is always physical. But then ethical teaching, whether in schools, or lecture-rooms, etc., is corrupted in its source. For it is not a matter of indifference by what motives or means one is led to a good purpose (the obedience to duty). However disgusting, then, metaphysics may appear to those pretended philosophers who dogmatize oracularly, or even brilliantly, about the doctrine of duty, it is, nevertheless, an indispensable duty for those who oppose it to go back to its principles even in ethics, and to begin by going to school on its benches.

We may fairly wonder how, after all previous explanations of the principles of duty, so far as it is derived from pure reason, it was still possible to reduce it again to a doctrine of happiness; in such a way, however, that a certain moral happiness not resting on empirical causes was ultimately arrived at, a self-contradictory nonentity. In fact, when the thinking man has conquered the temptations to vice, and is conscious of having done his (often hard) duty, he finds himself in a state of peace and satisfaction which may well be called happiness, in which virtue is her own reward. Now, says the eudaemonist, this delight, this happiness, is the real motive of his acting virtuously. The notion of duty, says be, does not immediately determine his will; it is only by means of the happiness in prospect that he is moved to his duty. Now, on the other hand, since he can promise himself this reward of virtue only from the consciousness of having done his duty, it is clear that the latter must have preceded: that is, be must feel himself bound to do his duty before he thinks, and without thinking, that happiness will be the consequence of obedience to duty. He is thus involved in a circle in his assignment of cause and effect. He can only hope to be happy if he is conscious of his obedience to duty: and he can only be moved to obedience to duty if be foresees that he will thereby become happy. But in this reasoning there is also a contradiction. For, on the one side, he must obey his duty, without asking what effect this will have on his happiness, consequently, from a moral principle; on the other side, he can only recognize something as his duty when he can reckon on happiness which will accrue to him thereby, and consequently on a pathological principle, which is the direct opposite of the former.

I have in another place (the Berlin Monatsschrift), reduced, as I believe, to the simplest expressions the distinction between pathological and moral pleasure. The pleasure, namely, which must precede the obedience to the law in order that one may act according to the law is pathological, and the process follows the physical order of nature; that which must be preceded by the law in order that it may be felt is in the moral order. If this distinction is not observed; if eudaemonism (the principle of happiness) is adopted as the principle instead of eleutheronomy (the principle of freedom of the inner legislation), the consequence is the euthanasia (quiet death) of all morality.

The cause of these mistakes is no other than the following: Those who are accustomed only to physiological explanations will not admit into their heads the categorical imperative from which these laws dictatorially proceed, notwithstanding that they feel themselves irresistibly forced by it. Dissatisfied at not being able to explain what lies wholly beyond that sphere, namely, freedom of the elective will, elevating as is this privilege, that man has of being capable of such an idea. They are stirred up by the proud claims of speculative reason, which feels its power so strongly in the fields, just as if they were allies leagued in defence of the omnipotence of theoretical reason and roused by a general call to arms to resist that idea; and thus they are at present, and perhaps for a long time to come, though ultimately in vain, to attack the moral concept of freedom and if possible render it doubtful.

INTRODUCTION

Introduction To The Metaphysical Elements Of Ethics

Ethics in ancient times signified moral philosophy (philosophia moral is) generally, which was also called the doctrine of duties. Subsequently it was found advisable to confine this name to a part of moral philosophy, namely, to the doctrine of duties which are not subject to external laws (for which in German the name Tugendlehre was found suitable). Thus the system of general deontology is divided into that of jurisprudence (jurisprudentia), which is capable of external laws, and of ethics, which is not thus capable, and we may let this division stand.

I. Exposition of the Conception of Ethics

The notion of duty is in itself already the notion of a constraint of the free elective will by the law; whether this constraint be an external one or be self-constraint. The moral imperative, by its categorical (the unconditional ought) announces this constraint, which therefore does not apply to all rational beings (for there may also be holy beings), but applies to men as rational physical beings who are unholy enough to be seduced by pleasure to the transgression of the moral law, although they themselves recognize its authority; and when they do obey it, to obey it unwillingly (with resistance of their inclination); and it is in this that the constraint properly consists.[2] Now, as man is a free (moral) being, the notion of duty can contain only self-constraint (by the idea of the law itself), when we look to the internal determination of the will (the spring), for thus only is it possible to combine that constraint (even if it were external) with the freedom of the elective will. The notion of duty then must be an ethical one.

The impulses of nature, then, contain hindrances to the fulfillment of duty in the mind of man, and resisting forces, some of them powerful; and he must judge himself

---

[2] Man, however, as at the same time a moral being, when he considers himself objectively, which he is qualified to do by his pure practical reason, (i.e., according to humanity in his own person). finds himself holy enough to transgress the law only unwillingly; for there is no man so depraved who in this transgression would not feel a resistance and an abhorrence of himself, so that he must put a force on himself. It is impossible to explain the phenomenon that at this parting of the ways (where the beautiful fable places Hercules between virtue and sensuality) man shows more propensity to obey inclination than the law. For, we can only explain what happens by tracing it to a cause according to physical laws; but then we should not be able to conceive the elective will as free. Now this mutually opposed self-constraint and the inevitability of it makes us recognize the incomprehensible property of freedom.

able to combat these and to conquer them by means of reason, not in the future, but in the present, simultaneously with the thought; he must judge that he can do what the law unconditionally commands that be ought.

Now the power and resolved purpose to resist a strong but unjust opponent is called fortitude (fortitudo), and when concerned with the opponent of the moral character within us, it is virtue (virtus, fortitudo moralis). Accordingly, general deontology, in that part which brings not external, but internal, freedom under laws is the doctrine of virtue.

Jurisprudence had to do only with the formal condition of external freedom (the condition of consistency with itself, if its maxim became a universal law), that is, with law. Ethics, on the contrary, supplies us with a matter (an object of the free elective will), an end of pure reason which is at the same time conceived as an objectively necessary end, i.e., as duty for all men. For, as the sensible inclinations mislead us to ends (which are the matter of the elective will) that may contradict duty, the legislating reason cannot otherwise guard against their influence than by an opposite moral end, which therefore must be given a priori independently on inclination.

An end is an object of the elective will (of a rational being) by the idea of which this will is determined to an action for the production of this object. Now I may be forced by others to actions which are directed to an end as means, but I cannot be forced to have an end; I can only make something an end to myself. If, however, I am also bound to make something which lies in the notions of practical reason an end to myself, and therefore besides the formal determining principle of the elective will (as contained in law) to have also a material principle, an end which can be opposed to the end derived from sensible impulses; then this gives the notion of an end which is in itself a duty. The doctrine of this cannot belong to jurisprudence, but to ethics, since this alone includes in its conception self-constraint according to moral laws.

For this reason, ethics may also be defined as the system of the ends of the pure practical reason. The two parts of moral philosophy are distinguished as treating respectively of ends and of duties of constraint. That ethics contains duties to the observance of which one cannot be (physically) forced by others, is merely the consequence of this, that it is a doctrine of ends, since to be forced to have ends or to set them before one's self is a contradiction.

Now that ethics is a doctrine of virtue (doctrina officiorum virtutis) follows from the definition of virtue given above compared with the obligation, the peculiarity of which has just been shown. There is in fact no other determination of the elective will, except that to an end, which in the very notion of it implies that I cannot even physically be forced to it by the elective will of others. Another may indeed force me to do something which is not my end (but only means to the end of another), but he cannot force me to make it my own end, and yet I can have no end except of my own making. The latter supposition would be a contradiction- an act of freedom which yet at the same time would not be free. But there is no contradiction in setting before one's self an end which is also a duty: for in this case I constrain myself, and this is quite consistent with freedom.[3] But how is such an end possible? That is now the question. For the possibility of the notion of the thing (viz., that it is not self-contradictory) is not enough to prove the possibility of the thing itself (the objective reality of the notion).

II. Exposition of the Notion of an End which is also a Duty

We can conceive the relation of end to duty in two ways; either starting from the end to find the maxim of the dutiful actions; or conversely, setting out from this to find the end which is also duty. jurisprudence proceeds in the former way. It is left to everyone's free elective will what end he will choose for his action. But its maxim is determined a priori; namely, that the freedom of the agent must be consistent with the freedom of every other according to a universal law.

Ethics, however, proceeds in the opposite way. It cannot start from the ends which the man may propose to himself, and hence give directions as to the maxims he should adopt, that is, as to his duty; for that would be to take empirical principles of maxims, and these could not give any notion of duty; since this, the categorical ought, has its root in pure reason alone. Indeed, if the maxims were to be adopted in accordance with those ends (which are all selfish), we could not properly speak of the notion of duty at all. Hence in ethics the notion of duty must lead to ends, and must on moral principles give the foundation of maxims with respect to the ends which we ought to propose to ourselves.

Setting aside the question what sort of end that is which is in itself a duty, and how such an end is possible, it is here only necessary to show that a duty of this kind is called a duty of virtue, and why it is so called.

To every duty corresponds a right of action (facultas moral is generatim), but all duties do not imply a corresponding right (facultas juridica) of another to compel any one, but only the duties called legal duties. Similarly to all ethical obligation corresponds the notion of virtue, but it does not follow that all ethical duties are duties of virtue. Those, in fact, are not so which do not concern so much a certain end (matter, object of the elective will), but merely that which is formal in the moral determination of the will (e.g., that the dutiful action must also be done from duty). It is only an end which is also duty that can be called a duty of virtue. Hence there are several of the latter kind (and thus there are distinct virtues); on the contrary, there is

---

[3] The less a man can be physically forced, and the more he can be morally forced (by the mere idea of duty), so much the freer he is. The man, for example, who is of sufficiently firm resolution and strong mind not to give up an enjoyment which he has resolved on, however much loss is shown as resulting there from, and who yet desists from his purpose unhesitatingly, though very reluctantly, when he finds that it would cause him to neglect an official duty or a sick father; this man proves his freedom in the highest degree by this very thing, that he cannot resist the voice of duty.

only one duty of the former kind, but it is one which is valid for all actions (only one virtuous disposition).

The duty of virtue is essentially distinguished from the duty of justice in this respect; that it is morally possible to be externally compelled to the latter, whereas the former rests on free self-constraint only. For finite holy beings (which cannot even be tempted to the violation of duty) there is no doctrine of virtue, but only moral philosophy, the latter being an autonomy of practical reason, whereas the former is also an autocracy of it. That is, it includes a consciousness- not indeed immediately perceived, but rightly concluded, from the moral categorical imperative- of the power to become master of one's inclinations which resist the law; so that human morality in its highest stage can yet be nothing more than virtue; even if it were quite pure (perfectly free from the influence of a spring foreign to duty), a state which is poetically personified under the name of the wise man (as an ideal to which one should continually approximate).

Virtue, however, is not to be defined and esteemed merely as habit, and (as it is expressed in the prize essay of Cochius) as a long custom acquired by practice of morally good actions. For, if this is not an effect of well-resolved and firm principles ever more and more purified, then, like any other mechanical arrangement brought about by technical practical reason, it is neither armed for all circumstances nor adequately secured against the change that may be wrought by new allurements.

REMARK

To virtue = + a is opposed as its logical contradictory (contradictorie oppositum) the negative lack of virtue (moral weakness) = o; but vice = a is its contrary (contrarie s. realiter oppositum); and it is not merely a needless question but an offensive one to ask whether great crimes do not perhaps demand more strength of mind than great virtues. For by strength of mind we understand the strength of purpose of a man, as a being endowed with freedom, and consequently so far as he is master of himself (in his senses) and therefore in a healthy condition of mind. But great crimes are paroxysms, the very sight of which makes the man of healthy mind shudder. The question would therefore be something like this: whether a man in a fit of madness can have more physical strength than if he is in his senses; and we may admit this without on that account ascribing to him more strength of mind, if by mind we understand the vital principle of man in the free use of his powers. For since those crimes have their ground merely in the power of the inclinations that weaken reason, which does not prove strength of mind, this question would be nearly the same as the question whether a man in a fit of illness can show more strength than in a healthy condition; and this may be directly denied, since the want of health, which consists in the proper balance of all the bodily forces of the man, is a weakness in the system of these forces, by which system alone we can estimate absolute health.

III. Of the Reason for conceiving an End which is also a Duty

An end is an object of the free elective will, the idea of which determines this will to an action by which the object is produced. Accordingly every action has its end, and as no one can have an end without himself making the object of his elective will his end, hence to have some end of actions is an act of the freedom of the agent, not an affect of physical nature. Now, since this act which determines an end is a practical principle which commands not the means (therefore not conditionally) but the end itself (therefore unconditionally), hence it is a categorical imperative of pure practical reason and one, therefore, which combines a concept of duty with that of an end in general.

Now there must be such an end and a categorical imperative corresponding to it. For since there are free actions, there must also be ends to which as an object those actions are directed. Amongst these ends there must also be some which are at the same time (that is, by their very notion) duties. For if there were none such, then since no actions can be without an end, all ends which practical reason might have would be valid only as means to other ends, and a categorical imperative would be impossible; a supposition which destroys all moral philosophy.

Here, therefore, we treat not of ends which man actually makes to himself in accordance with the sensible impulses of his nature, but of objects of the free elective will under its own laws- objects which he ought to make his end. We may call the former technical (subjective), properly pragmatical, including the rules of prudence in the choice of its ends; but the latter we must call the moral (objective) doctrine of ends. This distinction is, however, superfluous here, since moral philosophy already by its very notion is clearly separated from the doctrine of physical nature (in the present instance, anthropology). The latter resting on empirical principles, whereas the moral doctrine of ends which treats of duties rests on principles given a priori in pure practical reason.

IV. What are the Ends which are also Duties?

They are: A. OUR OWN PERFECTION, B. HAPPINESS OF OTHERS.

We cannot invert these and make on one side our own happiness, and on the other the perfection of others, ends which should be in themselves duties for the same person.

For one's own happiness is, no doubt, an end that all men have (by virtue of the impulse of their nature), but this end cannot without contradiction be regarded as a duty. What a man of himself inevitably wills does not come under the notion of duty, for this is a constraint to an end reluctantly adopted. It is, therefore, a contradiction to say that a man is in duty bound to advance his own happiness with all his power.

It is likewise a contradiction to make the perfection of another my end, and to regard myself as in duty bound to promote it. For it is just in this that the perfection of another man as a person consists, namely, that he is able of himself to set before him his own end according to his own notions of duty; and it is a contradiction to require (to make it a duty for me) that I should do something which no other but himself can do.

V. Explanation of these two Notions

A. OUR OWN PERFECTION

The word perfection is liable to many misconceptions. It is sometimes understood as a notion belonging to transcendental philosophy; viz., the notion of the totality of the manifold which taken together constitutes a thing; sometimes, again, it is understood as belonging to teleology, so that it signifies the correspondence of the properties of a thing to an end. Perfection in the former sense might be called quantitative (material), in the latter qualitative (formal) perfection. The former can be one only, for the whole of what belongs to the one thing is one. But of the latter there may be several in one thing; and it is of the latter property that we here treat.

When it is said of the perfection that belongs to man generally (properly speaking, to humanity), that it is in itself a duty to make this our end, it must be placed in that which may be the effect of one's deed, not in that which is merely an endowment for which we have to thank nature; for otherwise it would not be duty. Consequently, it can be nothing else than the cultivation of one's power (or natural capacity) and also of one's will (moral disposition) to satisfy the requirement of duty in general. The supreme element in the former (the power) is the understanding, it being the faculty of concepts, and, therefore, also of those concepts which refer to duty. First it is his duty to labour to raise himself out of the rudeness of his nature, out of his animal nature more and more to humanity, by which alone he is capable of setting before him ends to supply the defects of his ignorance by instruction, and to correct his errors; he is not merely counselled to do this by reason as technically practical, with a view to his purposes of other kinds (as art), but reason, as morally practical, absolutely commands him to do it, and makes this end his duty, in order that he may be worthy of the humanity that dwells in him. Secondly, to carry the cultivation of his will up to the purest virtuous disposition, that, namely, in which the law is also the spring of his dutiful actions, and to obey it from duty, for this is internal morally practical perfection. This is called the moral sense (as it were a special sense, sensus moralis), because it is a feeling of the effect which the legislative will within himself exercises on the faculty of acting accordingly. This is, indeed, often misused fanatically, as though (like the genius of Socrates) it preceded reason, or even could dispense with judgement of reason; but still it is a moral perfection, making every special end, which is also a duty, one's own end.

B. HAPPINESS OF OTHERS

It is inevitable for human nature that man should wish and seek for happiness, that is, satisfaction with his condition, with certainty of the continuance of this satisfaction. But for this very reason it is not an end that is also a duty. Some writers still make a distinction between moral and physical happiness (the former consisting in satisfaction with one's person and moral behavior, that is, with what one does; the other in satisfaction with that which nature confers, consequently with what one enjoys as a foreign gift). Without at present censuring the misuse of the word (which even involves a contradiction), it must be observed that the feeling of the former belongs solely to the preceding head, namely, perfection. For he who is to feel himself happy in the mere consciousness of his uprightness already possesses that perfection which in the previous section was defined as that end which is also duty.

If happiness, then, is in question, which it is to be my duty to promote as my end, it must be the happiness of other men whose (permitted) end I hereby make also mine. It still remains left to themselves to decide what they shall reckon as belonging to their happiness; only that it is in my power to decline many things which they so reckon, but which I do not so regard, supposing that they have no right to demand it from me as their own. A plausible objection often advanced against the division of duties above adopted consists in setting over against that end a supposed obligation to study my own (physical) happiness, and thus making this, which is my natural and merely subjective end, my duty (and objective end). This requires to be cleared up.

Adversity, pain, and want are great temptations to transgression of one's duty; accordingly it would seem that strength, health, a competence, and welfare generally, which are opposed to that influence, may also be regarded as ends that are also duties; that is, that it is a duty to promote our own happiness not merely to make that of others our end. But in that case the end is not happiness but the morality of the agent; and happiness is only the means of removing the hindrances to morality; permitted means, since no one has a right to demand from me the sacrifice of my not immoral ends. It is not directly a duty to seek a competence for one's self; but indirectly it may be so; namely, in order to guard against poverty which is a great temptation to vice. But then it is not my happiness but my morality, to maintain which in its integrity is at once my end and my duty.

VI. Ethics does not supply Laws for Actions (which is done by Jurisprudence), but only for the Maxims of Action

The notion of duty stands in immediate relation to a law (even though I abstract from every end which is the matter of the law); as is shown by the formal principle of duty in the categorical imperative: "Act so that the maxims of thy action might become a universal law." But in ethics this is conceived as the law of thy own will, not of will in general, which might be that of others; for in the latter case it would give rise to a judicial duty which does not belong to the domain of ethics. In ethics, maxims are regarded as those subjective laws which merely have the specific character of universal legislation, which is only a negative principle (not to contradict a law in general). How, then, can there be further a law for the maxims of actions?

It is the notion of an end which is also a duty, a notion peculiar to ethics, that alone is the foundation of a law for the maxims of actions; by making the subjective end (that which every one has) subordinate to the objective end (that which every one ought to make his own). The imperative: "Thou shalt make this or that thy end (e. g., the happiness of others)" applies to the matter of the elective will (an object). Now since no free action is possible, without the agent having in view in it some end (as matter of his elective will), it follows that, if there is an end which is also a duty, the maxims of actions which are means to ends must contain only the condition of fitness for a possible universal legislation: on the other hand, the end which is also a duty can make it a law that we should have such a maxim, whilst for the maxim itself the possibility of agreeing with a universal legislation is sufficient.

For maxims of actions may be arbitrary, and are only limited by the condition of fitness for a universal legislation, which is the formal principle of actions. But a law abolishes the arbitrary character of actions, and is by this distinguished from recommendation (in which one only desires to know the best means to an end).

VII. Ethical Duties are of indeterminate, Juridical Duties of strict, Obligation

This proposition is a consequence of the foregoing; for if the law can only command the maxim of the actions, not the actions themselves, this is a sign that it leaves in the observance of it a latitude (latitudo) for the elective will; that is, it cannot definitely assign how and how much we should do by the action towards the end which is also duty. But by an indeterminate duty is not meant a permission to make exceptions from the maxim of the actions, but only the permission to limit one maxim of duty by another (e. g., the general love of our neighbor by the love of parents); and this in fact enlarges the field for the practice of virtue. The more indeterminate the duty, and the more imperfect accordingly the obligation of the man to the action, and the closer he nevertheless brings this maxim of obedience thereto (in his own mind) to the strict duty (of justice), so much the more perfect is his virtuous action.

Hence it is only imperfect duties that are duties of virtue. The fulfillment of them is merit (meritum) = + a; but their transgression is not necessarily demerit (demeritum) = - a, but only moral unworth = o, unless the agent made it a principle not to conform to those duties. The strength of purpose in the former case is alone properly called virtue [Tugend] (virtus); the weakness in the latter case is not vice (vitium), but rather only lack of virtue [Untugend], a want of moral strength (defectus moralis). (As the word Tugend is derived from taugen [to be good for something], Untugend by its etymology signifies good for nothing.) Every action contrary to duty is called transgression (peccatum). Deliberate transgression which has become a principle is what properly constitutes what is called vice (vitium).

Although the conformity of actions to justice (i.e., to be an upright man) is nothing meritorious, yet the conformity of the maxim of such actions regarded as duties, that is, reverence for justice is meritorious. For by this the man makes the right of humanity or of men his own end, and thereby enlarges his notion of duty beyond that of indebtedness (officium debiti), since although another man by virtue of his rights can demand that my actions shall conform to the law, he cannot demand that the law shall also contain the spring of these actions. The same thing is true of the general ethical command, "Act dutifully from a sense of duty." To fix this disposition firmly in one's mind and to quicken it is, as in the former case, meritorious, because it goes beyond the law of duty in actions and makes the law in itself the spring.

But just for or reason, those duties also must be reckoned as of indeterminate obligation, in respect of which there exists a subjective principle which ethically rewards them; or to bring them as near as possible to the notion of a strict obligation, a principle of susceptibility of this reward according to the law of virtue; namely, a moral pleasure which goes beyond mere satisfaction with oneself (which may be merely negative), and of which it is proudly said that in this consciousness virtue is its own reward.

When this merit is a merit of the man in respect of other men of promoting their natural ends, which are recognized as such by all men (making their happiness his own), we might call it the sweet merit, the consciousness of which creates a moral enjoyment in which men are by sympathy inclined to revel; whereas the bitter merit of promoting the true welfare of other men, even though they should not recognize it as such (in the case of the unthankful and ungrateful), has commonly no such reaction, but only produces a satisfaction with one's self, although in the latter case this would be even greater.

VIII. Exposition of the Duties of Virtue as Intermediate Duties

(1) OUR OWN PERFECTION as an end which is also a duty

(a) Physical perfection; that is, cultivation of all our faculties generally for the promotion of the ends set before us by reason. That this is a duty, and therefore an end in itself, and that the effort to effect this even without regard to the advantage that it secures us, is based, not on a conditional (pragmatic), but an unconditional (moral) imperative, may be seen from the following consideration. The power of proposing to ourselves an end is the characteristic of humanity (as distinguished from the brutes). With the end of humanity in our own person is therefore combined the rational will, and consequently the duty of deserving well of humanity by culture generally, by acquiring or advancing the power to carry out all sorts of possible ends, so far as this power is to be found in man; that is, it is a duty to cultivate the crude capacities of our nature, since it is by that cultivation that the animal is raised to man, therefore it is a duty in itself.

This duty, however, is merely ethical, that is, of indeterminate obligation. No principle of reason prescribes how far one must go in this effort (in enlarging or correcting his faculty of understanding, that is, in acquisition of knowledge or technical capacity); and besides the difference in the circumstances into which men may come makes the choice of the kind of employment for which he should cultivate his talent very arbitrary. Here, therefore, there is no law of reason for actions, but only for the maxim of actions, viz.: "Cultivate thy faculties of mind and body so as to be effective for all ends that may come in thy way, uncertain which of them may become thy own."

(b) Cultivation of Morality in ourselves. The greatest moral perfection of man is to do his duty, and that from duty (that the law be not only the rule but also the spring of his actions). Now at first sight this seems to be a strict obligation, and as if the principle of duty commanded not merely the legality of every action, but also the morality, i.e., the mental disposition, with the exactness and strictness of a law; but in fact the law commands even here only the maxim of the action, namely, that we should seek the ground of obligation, not in the sensible impulses (advantage or disadvantage), but wholly in the law; so that the action itself is not commanded. For it is not possible to man to see so far into the depth of his own heart that he could ever be thoroughly certain of the purity of his moral purpose and the sincerity of his mind even in one single action, although he has no doubt about the legality of it. Nay, often the weakness which deters a man from the risk of a crime is regarded by him as virtue (which gives the notion of strength). And how many there are who may have led a long blameless life, who are only fortunate in having escaped so many temptations. How much of the element of pure morality in their mental disposition may have belonged to each deed remains hidden even from themselves.

Accordingly, this duty to estimate the worth of one's actions not merely by their legality, but also by their morality (mental disposition), is only of indeterminate obligation; the law does not command this internal action in the human mind itself, but only the maxim of the action, namely, that we should strive with all our power that for all dutiful actions the thought of duty should be of itself an adequate spring.

(2) HAPPINESS OF OTHERS as an end which is also a duty

(a) Physical Welfare. Benevolent wishes may be unlimited, for they do not imply doing anything. But the case is more difficult with benevolent action, especially when this is to be done, not from friendly inclination (love) to others, but from duty, at the expense of the sacrifice and mortification of many of our appetites. That this beneficence is a duty results from this: that since our self-love cannot be separated from the need to be loved by others (to obtain help from them in case of necessity), we therefore make ourselves an end for others; and this maxim can never be obligatory except by having the specific character of a universal law, and consequently by means of a will that we should also make others our ends. Hence the happiness of others is an end that is also a duty.

I am only bound then to sacrifice to others a part of my welfare without hope of recompense: because it is my duty, and it is impossible to assign definite limits how far that may go. Much depends on what would be the true want of each according to his own feelings, and it must be left to each to determine this for himself. For that one should sacrifice his own happiness, his true wants, in order to promote that of others, would be a self-contradictory maxim if made a universal law. This duty, therefore, is only indeterminate; it has a certain latitude within which one may do more or less without our being able to assign its limits definitely. The law holds only for the maxims, not for definite actions.

(b) Moral well-being of others (salus moral is) also belongs to the happiness of others, which it is our duty to promote, but only a negative duty. The pain that a man feels from remorse of conscience, although its origin is moral, is yet in its operation physical, like grief, fear, and every other diseased condition. To take care that he should not be deservedly smitten by this inward reproach is not indeed my duty but his business; nevertheless, it is my duty to do nothing which by the nature of man might seduce him to that for which his conscience may hereafter torment him, that is, it is my duty not to give him occasion of stumbling. But there are no definite limits within which this care for the moral satisfaction of others must be kept; therefore it involves only an indeterminate obligation.

IX. What is a Duty of Virtue?

Virtue is the strength of the man's maxim in his obedience to duty. All strength is known only by the obstacles that it can overcome; and in the case of virtue the obstacles are the natural inclinations which may come into conflict with the moral purpose; and as it is the man who himself puts these obstacles in the way of his maxims, hence virtue is not merely a self-constraint (for that might be an effort of one inclination to constrain another), but is also a constraint according to a principle of inward freedom, and therefore by the mere idea of duty, according to its formal law.

All duties involve a notion of necessitation by the law, and ethical duties involve a necessitation for which only an internal legislation is possible; juridical duties, on the other hand, one for which external legislation also is possible. Both, therefore, include the notion of constraint, either self-constraint or constraint by others. The moral power of the former is virtue, and the action springing from such a disposition (from reverence for the law) may be called a virtuous action (ethical), although the law expresses a juridical duty. For it is the doctrine of virtue that commands us to regard the rights of men as holy.

But it does not follow that everything the doing of which is virtue, is, properly speaking, a duty of virtue. The former may concern merely the form of the maxims; the latter applies to the matter of them, namely, to an end which is also conceived as duty. Now, as the ethical obligation to ends, of which there may be many, is only indeterminate, because it contains only a law for the maxim of actions, and the end is the matter (object) of elective will; hence there are many duties, differing according to the difference of lawful ends, which may be called duties of virtue (officia honestatis), just because they are subject only to free self-constraint, not to the constraint of other men, and determine the end which is also a duty.

Virtue, being a coincidence of the rational will, with every duty firmly settled in the character, is, like everything formal, only one and the same. But, as regards the end of actions, which is also duty, that is, as regards the matter which one ought to make an end, there may be several virtues; and as the obligation to its maxim is called a duty of virtue, it follows that there are also several duties of virtue.

The supreme principle of ethics (the doctrine of virtue) is: "Act on a maxim, the ends of which are such as it might be a universal law for everyone to have." On this principle a man is an end to himself as well as others, and it is not enough that he is not permitted to use either himself or others merely as means (which would imply that be might be indifferent to them), but it is in itself a duty of every man to make mankind in general his end.

The principle of ethics being a categorical imperative does not admit of proof, but it admits of a justification from principles of pure practical reason. Whatever in relation to mankind, to oneself, and others, can be an end, that is an end for pure practical reason: for this is a faculty of assigning ends in general; and to be indifferent to them, that is, to take no interest in them, is a contradiction; since in that case it would not determine the maxims of actions (which always involve an end), and consequently would cease to be practical reasons. Pure reason, however, cannot command any ends a priori, except so far as it declares the same to be also a duty, which duty is then cared a duty of virtue.

X. The Supreme Principle of Jurisprudence was Analytical; that of Ethics is Synthetical

That external constraint, so far as it withstands that which hinders the external freedom that agrees with general laws (as an obstacle of the obstacle thereto), can be consistent with ends generally, is clear on the principle of contradiction, and I need not go beyond the notion of freedom in order to see it, let the end which each may be what he will. Accordingly, the supreme principle of jurisprudence is an analytical principle. On the contrary the principle of ethics goes beyond the notion of external freedom and, by general laws, connects further with it an end which it makes a duty. This principle, therefore, is synthetic. The possibility of it is contained in the deduction (SS ix).

This enlargement of the notion of duty beyond that of external freedom and of its limitation by the merely formal condition of its constant harmony; this, I say, in which, instead of constraint from without, there is set up freedom within, the power of self-constraint, and that not by the help of other inclinations, but by pure practical reason (which scorns all such help), consists in this fact, which raises it above juridical duty; that by it ends are proposed from which jurisprudence altogether abstracts. In the case of the moral imperative, and the supposition of freedom which it necessarily involves, the law, the power (to fulfil it) and the rational will that determines the maxim, constitute all the elements that form the notion of juridical duty. But in the imperative, which commands the duty of virtue, there is added, besides the notion of self-constraint, that of an end; not one that we have, but that we ought to have, which, therefore, pure practical reason has in itself, whose highest, unconditional end (which, however, continues to be duty) consists in this: that virtue is its own end and, by deserving well of men, is also its own reward. Herein it shines so brightly as an ideal to human perceptions, it seems to cast in the shade even holiness itself, which is never tempted to transgression.[4] This, however, is an illusion arising from the fact that as we have no measure for the degree of strength, except the greatness of the obstacles which might have been overcome (which in our case are the inclinations), we are led to mistake the subjective conditions of estimation of a magnitude for the objective conditions of the magnitude itself. But when compared with human ends, all of which have their obstacles to be overcome, it is true that the worth of virtue itself, which is its own end, far outweighs the worth of all the utility and all the empirical ends and advantages which it may have as consequences.

We may, indeed, say that man is obliged to virtue (as a moral strength). For although the power (facultas) to overcome all imposing sensible impulses by virtue of his freedom can and must be presupposed, yet this power regarded as strength (robur) is something that must be acquired by the moral spring (the idea of the law) being elevated by contemplation of the dignity of the pure law of reason in us, and at the same time also by exercise.

XI. According to the preceding Principles, the Scheme of Duties of Virtue may be thus exhibited

The Material Element of the Duty of Virtue

1	2
Internal Duty of Virtue	*External Virtue of Duty*
My Own End, which is also my Duty	The End of Others, the promotion of which is also my Duty
(My own Perfection)	(The Happiness of Others)

---

[4] So that one might very two well-known lines of Haller thus:

With all his failings, man is still
Better than angels void of will.

3	4
The Law which is also Spring On which the Morality	The End which is also Spring On which the Legality

of every free determination of will rests the Formal Element of the Duty of Virtue.

XII. Preliminary Notions of the Susceptibility of the Mind for Notions of Duty Generally

These are such moral qualities, as when a man does not possess them, he is not bound to acquire them. They are: the moral feeling, conscience, love of one's neighbour, and respect for ourselves (self-esteem). There is no obligation to have these, since they are subjective conditions of susceptibility for the notion of duty, not objective conditions of morality. They are all sensitive and antecedent, but natural capacities of mind (praedispositio) to be affected by notions of duty; capacities which it cannot be regarded as a duty to have, but which every man has, and by virtue of which he can be brought under obligation. The consciousness of them is not of empirical origin, but can only follow on that of a moral law, as an effect of the same on the mind.

A. THE MORAL FEELING

This is the susceptibility for pleasure or displeasure, merely from the consciousness of the agreement or disagreement of our action with the law of duty. Now, every determination of the elective will proceeds from the idea of the possible action through the feeling of pleasure or displeasure in taking an interest in it or its effect to the deed; and here the sensitive state (the affection of the internal sense) is either a pathological or a moral feeling. The former is the feeling that precedes the idea of the law, the latter that which may follow it.

Now it cannot be a duty to have a moral feeling, or to acquire it; for all consciousness of obligation supposes this feeling in order that one may become conscious of the necessitation that lies in the notion of duty; but every man (as a moral being) has it originally in himself; the obligation, then, can only extend to the cultivation of it and the strengthening of it even by admiration of its inscrutable origin; and this is effected by showing how it is just, by the mere conception of reason, that it is excited most strongly, in its own purity and apart from every pathological stimulus; and it is improper to call this feeling a moral sense; for the word sense generally means a theoretical power of perception directed to an object; whereas the moral feeling (like pleasure and displeasure in general) is something merely subjective, which supplies no knowledge. No man is wholly destitute of moral feeling, for if he were totally unsusceptible of this sensation he would be morally dead; and, to speak in the language of physicians, if the moral vital force could no longer produce any effect on this feeling, then his humanity would be dissolved (as it were by chemical laws) into mere animality and be irrevocably confounded with the mass of other physical beings. But we have no special sense for (moral) good and evil any more than for truth, although such expressions are often used; but we have a susceptibility of the free elective will for being moved by pure practical reason and its law; and it is this that we call the moral feeling.

B. OF CONSCIENCE

Similarly, conscience is not a thing to be acquired, and it is not a duty to acquire it; but every man, as a moral being, has it originally within him. To be bound to have a conscience would be as much as to say to be under a duty to recognize duties. For conscience is practical reason which, in every case of law, holds before a man his duty for acquittal or condemnation; consequently it does not refer to an object, but only to the subject (affecting the moral feeling by its own act); so that it is an inevitable fact, not an obligation and duty. When, therefore, it is said, "This man has no conscience," what is meant is that he pays no heed to its dictates. For if he really had none, he would not take credit to himself for anything done according to duty, nor reproach himself with violation of duty, and therefore he would be unable even to conceive the duty of having a conscience.

I pass by the manifold subdivisions of conscience, and only observe what follows from what has just been said, namely, that there is no such thing as an erring conscience. No doubt it is possible sometimes to err in the objective judgement whether something is a duty or not; but I cannot err in the subjective whether I have compared it with my practical (here judicially acting) reason for the purpose of that judgement: for if I erred I would not have exercised practical judgement at all, and in that case there is neither truth nor error. Unconscientiousness is not want of conscience, but the propensity not to heed its judgement. But when a man is conscious of having acted according to his conscience, then, as far as regards guilt or innocence, nothing more can be required of him, only he is bound to enlighten his understanding as to what is duty or not; but when it comes or has come to action, then conscience speaks involuntarily and inevitably. To act conscientiously can, therefore, not be a duty, since otherwise it would be necessary to have a second conscience, in order to be conscious of the act of the first.

The duty here is only to cultivate our conscience, to quicken our attention to the voice of the internal judge, and to use all means to secure obedience to it, and is thus our indirect duty.

C. OF LOVE TO MEN

Love is a matter of feeling, not of will or volition, and I cannot love because I will to do so, still less because I ought (I cannot be necessitated to love); hence there is no such thing as a duty to love. Benevolence, however (amor benevolentiae), as a mode of action, may be subject to a law of duty. Disinterested benevolence is often called (though very improperly) love; even where the happiness of the other is not concerned, but the complete and free surrender of all one's own ends to the ends of another (even a superhuman) being, love is spoken of as being also our duty. But all duty is necessitation or constraint, although it may be self-constraint according to a law. But what is done from constraint is not done from love.

It is a duty to do good to other men according to our power, whether we love them or not, and this duty loses nothing of its weight, although we must make the sad remark that our species, alas! is not such as to be found particularly worthy of love when we know it more closely. Hatred of men, however, is always hateful: even though without any active hostility it consists only in complete aversion from mankind (the solitary misanthropy). For benevolence still remains a duty even towards the man-hater, whom one cannot love, but to whom we can show kindness.

To hate vice in men is neither duty nor against duty, but a mere feeling of horror of vice, the will having no influence on the feeling nor the feeling on the will. Beneficence is a duty. He who often practises this, and sees his beneficent purpose succeed, comes at last really to love him whom he has benefited. When, therefore, it is said: "Thou shalt love thy neighbour as thyself," this does not mean, "Thou shalt first of all love, and by means of this love (in the next place) do him good"; but: "Do good to thy neighbour, and this beneficence will produce in thee the love of men (as a settled habit of inclination to beneficence)."

The love of complacency (amor complacentiae,) would therefore alone be direct. This is a pleasure immediately connected with the idea of the existence of an object, and to have a duty to this, that is, to be necessitated to find pleasure in a thing, is a contradiction.

D. OF RESPECT

Respect (reverentia) is likewise something merely subjective; a feeling of a peculiar kind not a judgement about an object which it would be a duty to effect or to advance. For if considered as duty it could only be conceived as such by means of the respect which we have for it. To have a duty to this, therefore, would be as much as to say to be bound in duty to have a duty. When, therefore, it is said: "Man has a duty of self-esteem," this is improperly stated, and we ought rather to say: "The law within him inevitably forces from him respect for his own being, and this feeling (which is of a peculiar kind) is a basis of certain duties, that is, of certain actions which may be consistent with his duty to himself." But we cannot say that he has a duty of respect for himself; for he must have respect for the law within himself, in order to be able to conceive duty at all.

XIII. General Principles of the Metaphysics of Morals in the treatment of Pure Ethics

First. A duty can have only a single ground of obligation; and if two or more proof of it are adduced, this is a certain mark that either no valid proof has yet been given, or that there are several distinct duties which have been regarded as one.

For all moral proofs, being philosophical, can only be drawn by means of rational knowledge from concepts, not like mathematics, through the construction of concepts. The latter science admits a variety of proofs of one and the same theorem; because in intuition a priori there may be several properties of an object, all of which lead back to the very same principle. If, for instance, to prove the duty of veracity, an argument is drawn first from the harm that a lie causes to other men; another from the worthlessness of a liar and the violation of his own self-respect, what is proved in the former argument is a duty of benevolence, not of veracity, that is to say, not the duty which required to be proved, but a different one. Now, if, in giving a variety of proof for one and the same theorem, we flatter ourselves that the multitude of reasons will compensate the lack of weight in each taken separately, this is a very unphilosophical resource, since it betrays trickery and dishonesty; for several insufficient proofs placed beside one another do not produce certainty, nor even probability. They should advance as reason and consequence in a series, up to the sufficient reason, and it is only in this way that they can have the force of proof. Yet the former is the usual device of the rhetorician.

Secondly. The difference between virtue and vice cannot be sought in the degree in which certain maxims are followed, but only in the specific quality of the maxims (their relation to the law). In other words, the vaunted principle of Aristotle, that virtue is the mean between two vices, is false.[5] For instance, suppose that good management is given as the mean between two vices, prodigality and avarice; then its origin as a virtue can neither be defined as the gradual diminution of the former vice (by saving), nor as the increase of the expenses of the miserly. These vices, in fact,

---

[5] The common classical formulae of ethics- medio tutissimus ibis; omne mimium vertitur in vitium; est modus in rebus, etc., medium tenuere beati; virtus est medium vitiorum et utrinque reductum- ["You will go most safely in the middle" (Virgil); "Every excess develops into a vice"; "There is a mean in all things, etc." (Horace); "Happy they who steadily pursue a middle course"; "Virtue is the mean between two vices and equally removed from either" (Horace).]- contain a poor sort of wisdom, which has no definite principles; for this mean between two extremes, who will assign it for me? Avarice (as a vice) is not distinguished from frugality (as a virtue) by merely being the lat pushed too far; but has a quite different principle; (maxim), namely placing the end of economy not in the enjoyment of one's means, but in the mere possession of them, renouncing enjoyment; just as the vice of prodigality is not to be sought in the excessive enjoyment of one's means, but in the bad maxim which makes the use of them, without regard to their maintenance, the sole end.

cannot be viewed as if they, proceeding as it were in opposite directions, met together in good management; but each of them has its own maxim, which necessarily contradicts that of the other.

For the same reason, no vice can be defined as an excess in the practice of certain actions beyond what is proper (e.g., Prodigalitas est excessus in consumendis opibus); or, as a less exercise of them than is fitting (Avaritia est defectus, etc.). For since in this way the degree is left quite undefined, and the question whether conduct accords with duty or not, turns wholly on this, such an account is of no use as a definition.

Thirdly. Ethical virtue must not be estimated by the power we attribute to man of fulfilling the law; but, conversely, the moral power must be estimated by the law, which commands categorically; not, therefore, by the empirical knowledge that we have of men as they are, but by the rational knowledge how, according to the ideas of humanity, they ought to be. These three maxims of the scientific treatment of ethics are opposed to the older apophthegms:

1. There is only one virtue and only one vice.

2. Virtue is the observance of the mean path between two opposite vices.

3. Virtue (like prudence) must be learned from experience.

XIV. Of Virtue in General

Virtue signifies a moral strength of will. But this does not exhaust the notion; for such strength might also belong to a holy (superhuman) being, in whom no opposing impulse counteracts the law of his rational will; who therefore willingly does everything in accordance with the law. Virtue then is the moral strength of a man's will in his obedience to duty; and this is a moral necessitation by his own law giving reason, inasmuch as this constitutes itself a power executing the law. It is not itself a duty, nor is it a duty to possess it (otherwise we should be in duty bound to have a duty), but it commands, and accompanies its command with a moral constraint (one possible by laws of internal freedom). But since this should be irresistible, strength is requisite, and the degree of this strength can be estimated only by the magnitude of the hindrances which man creates for himself, by his inclinations. Vices, the brood of unlawful dispositions, are the monsters that he has to combat; wherefore this moral strength as fortitude (fortitudo moral is) constitutes the greatest and only true martial glory of man; it is also called the true wisdom, namely, the practical, because it makes the ultimate end of the existence of man on earth its own end. Its possession alone makes man free, healthy, rich, a king, etc., nor either chance or fate deprive him of this, since he possesses himself, and the virtuous cannot lose his virtue.

All the encomiums bestowed on the ideal of humanity in its moral perfection can lose nothing of their practical reality by the examples of what men now are, have been, or will probably be hereafter; anthropology which proceeds from mere empirical knowledge cannot impair anthroponomy which is erected by the unconditionally legislating reason; and although virtue may now and then be called meritorious (in relation to men, not to the law), and be worthy of reward, yet in itself, as it is its own end, so also it must be regarded as its own reward.

Virtue considered in its complete perfection is, therefore, regarded not as if man possessed virtue, but as if virtue possessed the man, since in the former case it would appear as though he had still had the choice (for which he would then require another virtue, in order to select virtue from all other wares offered to him). To conceive a plurality of virtues (as we unavoidably must) is nothing else but to conceive various moral objects to which the (rational) will is led by the single principle of virtue; and it is the same with the opposite vices. The expression which personifies both is a contrivance for affecting the sensibility, pointing, however, to a moral sense. Hence it follows that an aesthetic of morals is not a part, but a subjective exposition of the Metaphysic of Morals; in which the emotions that accompany the force of the moral law make the that force to be felt; for example: disgust, horror, etc., which gives a sensible moral aversion in order to gain the precedence from the merely sensible incitement.

XV. Of the Principle on which Ethics is separated from Jurisprudence

This separation on which the subdivision of moral philosophy in general rests, is founded on this: that the notion of freedom, which is common to both, makes it necessary to divide duties into those of external and those of internal freedom; the latter of which alone are ethical. Hence this internal freedom which is the condition of all ethical duty must be discussed as a preliminary (discursus praeliminaris), just as above the doctrine of conscience was discussed as the condition of all duty.

REMARKS

Of the Doctrine of Virtue on the Principle Of Internal Freedom

Habit (habitus) is a facility of action and a subjective perfection of the elective will. But not every such facility is a free habit (habitus libertatis); for if it is custom (assuetudo), that is, a uniformity of action which, by frequent repetition, has become a necessity, then it is not a habit proceeding from freedom, and therefore not a moral habit. Virtue therefore cannot be defined as a habit of free law-abiding actions, unless indeed we add "determining itself in its action by the idea of the law"; and then this habit is not a property of the elective will, but of the rational will, which is a faculty that in adopting a rule also declares it to be a universal law, and it is only such a habit that can be reckoned as virtue. Two things are required for internal freedom: to be master of oneself in a given case (animus sui compos) and to have command over oneself (imperium in semetipsum), that is to subdue his emotions and to govern his passions. With these conditions, the character (indoles) is noble (erecta); in the opposite case, it is ignoble (indoles abjecta serva).

XVI. Virtue requires, first of all, Command over Oneself

Emotions and passions are essentially distinct; the former belong to feeling in so far as this coming before reflection makes it more difficult or even impossible. Hence emotion is called hasty (animus praeceps). And reason declares through the notion of virtue that a man should collect himself; but this weakness in the life of one's understanding, joined with the strength of a mental excitement, is only a lack of virtue (Untugend), and as it were a weak and childish thing, which may very well consist with the best will, and has further this one good thing in it, that this storm soon subsides. A propensity to emotion (e.g., resentment) is therefore not so closely related to vice as passion is. Passion, on the other hand, is the sensible appetite grown into a permanent inclination (e. g., hatred in contrast to resentment). The calmness with which one indulges it leaves room for reflection and allows the mind to frame principles thereon for itself; and thus when the inclination falls upon what contradicts the law, to brood on it, to allow it to root itself deeply, and thereby to take up evil (as of set purpose) into one's maxim; and this is then specifically evil, that is, it is a true vice.

Virtue, therefore, in so far as it is based on internal freedom, contains a positive command for man, namely, that he should bring all his powers and inclinations under his rule (that of reason); and this is a positive precept of command over himself which is additional to the prohibition, namely, that he should not allow himself to be governed by his feelings and inclinations (the duty of apathy); since, unless reason takes the reins of government into its own hands, the feelings and inclinations play the master over the man.

XVII. Virtue necessarily presupposes Apathy (considered as Strength)

This word (apathy) has come into bad repute, just as if it meant want of feeling, and therefore subjective indifference with respect to the objects of the elective will; it is supposed to be a weakness. This misconception may be avoided by giving the name moral apathy to that want of emotion which is to be distinguished from indifference. In the former, the feelings arising from sensible impressions lose their influence on the moral feeling only because the respect for the law is more powerful than all of them together. It is only the apparent strength of a fever patient that makes even the lively sympathy with good rise to an emotion, or rather degenerate into it. Such an emotion is called enthusiasm, and it is with reference to this that we are to explain the moderation which is usually recommended in virtuous practices:

Insani sapiens nomen ferat, aequus uniqui
Ultra quam satis est virtutem si petat ipsam.[6]

For otherwise it is absurd to imagine that one could be too wise or too virtuous. The emotion always belongs to the sensibility, no matter by what sort of object it may be excited. The true strength of virtue is the mind at rest, with a firm, deliberate resolution to bring its law into practice. That is the state of health in the moral life; on the contrary, the emotion, even when it is excited by the idea of the good, is a momentary glitter which leaves exhaustion after it. We may apply the term fantastically virtuous to the man who will admit nothing to be indifferent in respect of morality (adiaphora), and who strews all his steps with duties, as with traps, and will not allow it to be indifferent whether a man eats fish or flesh, drink beer or wine, when both agree with him; a micrology which, if adopted into the doctrine of virtue, would make its rule a tyranny.

REMARK

Virtue is always in progress, and yet always begins from the beginning. The former follows from the fact that, objectively considered, it is an ideal and unattainable, and yet it is a duty constantly to approximate to it. The second is founded subjectively on the nature of man which is affected by inclinations, under the influence of which virtue, with its maxims adopted once for all, can never settle in a position of rest; but, if it is not rising, inevitably falls; because moral maxims cannot, like technical, be based on custom (for this belongs to the physical character of the determination of will); but even if the practice of them become a custom, the agent would thereby lose the freedom in the choice of his maxims, which freedom is the character of an action done from duty.

ON CONSCIENCE

The consciousness of an internal tribunal in man (before which "his thoughts accuse or excuse one another") is CONSCIENCE.

Every man has a conscience, and finds himself observed by an inward judge which threatens and keeps him in awe (reverence combined with fear); and this power which watches over the laws within him is not something which he himself (arbitrarily) makes, but it is incorporated in his being. It follows him like his shadow, when he thinks to escape. He may indeed stupefy himself with pleasures and distractions, but cannot avoid now and then coming to himself or awaking, and then he at once perceives its awful voice. In his utmost depravity, he may, indeed, pay no attention to it, but he cannot avoid hearing it.

---

[6] Horace. ["Let the wise man bear the name of fool, and the just of unjust, if he pursue virtue herself beyond the proper bounds."]

Now this original intellectual and (as a conception of duty) moral capacity, called conscience, has this peculiarity in it, that although its business is a business of man with himself, yet he finds himself compelled by his reason to transact it as if at the command of another person. For the transaction here is the conduct of a trial (causa) before a tribunal. But that he who is accused by his conscience should be conceived as one and the same person with the judge is an absurd conception of a judicial court; for then the complainant would always lose his case. Therefore, in all duties the conscience of the man must regard another than himself as the judge of his actions, if it is to avoid self-contradiction. Now this other may be an actual or a merely ideal person which reason frames to itself. Such an idealized person (the authorized judge of conscience) must be one who knows the heart; for the tribunal is set up in the inward part of man; at the same time he must also be all-obliging, that is, must be or be conceived as a person in respect of whom all duties are to be regarded as his commands; since conscience is the inward judge of all free actions. Now, since such a moral being must at the same time possess all power (in heaven and earth), since otherwise he could not give his commands their proper effect (which the office of judge necessarily requires), and since such a moral being possessing power over all is called GOD, hence conscience must be conceived as the subjective principle of a responsibility for one's deeds before God; nay, this latter concept is contained (though it be only obscurely) in every moral self-consciousness.

THE END

Also From Merchant Books

Lightning Source UK Ltd.
Milton Keynes UK
20 November 2009

146471UK00001BC/94/P